COOK.
EAT.
LOVE.

FEARNE COTTON

COOK.
EAT.
LOVE.

Simple, nourishing recipes
for health and happiness

For Mum and Dad, and anyone else who spends 98% of their life thinking about food.

CONTENTS

WELCOME BACK TO MY KITCHEN! 6

MY STORE CUPBOARD 8

BREAKFAST 12

ELEVENSES 34

SOUPS AND SALADS 50

LUNCH ON THE RUN 76

AFTERNOON TREATS 98

FAMILY FAVOURITES 122

FOOD TO SHARE 148

DESSERTS 172

BAKED GOODIES 196

INDEX 216

ACKNOWLEDGEMENTS 223

WELCOME BACK TO MY KITCHEN!

It's still as messy, noisy and generally chaotic as ever, but – if possible – even more drenched in love. If you were one of the glorious humans who took a punt on my first cookbook, *Cook Happy, Cook Healthy*, then THANK YOU. Since finishing my first book my head has been spinning with new ideas, which I'm thrilled to share with you in this NEW book, *Cook. Eat. Love*.

Cooking brings me such vast amounts of joy – from the creation of a recipe and the alchemy of certain foods marrying so beautifully, to eating every mouthful with a smile on my face. I'm quite obviously not a trained chef but a highly enthusiastic home cook who loves nothing more than to experiment, create and feed my loved ones with delicious and wholesome, nurturing food. I adore how eating brings people together, be it as an intimate and much-needed hiatus during a busy day or in the throes of a bustling party where the ritual of dining gathers people together. It's the meeting of minds, mouths and rumbling tummies in a ceremonial thrice-daily interlude, which I never tire of.

These days I work most of my day around food and cooking, and can happily spend hours dreaming up or creating different dishes. How my body and my family operate are of paramount importance to me: I want us all to have optimum energy levels every day. I can't afford to have energy highs and lows rocketing me along an adrenalin-fuelled rollercoaster, as I did in my twenties.

Now I prefer a much calmer approach to life, and this book mirrors my passion for balance and nurturing. Life is so fast-paced for us all, with work, family, stress and worry. Looking after ourselves properly sometimes gets put to the back of the queue, or is viewed as a luxury. But eating well is a very simple, yet extremely effective, way of ensuring we all get what we need to continue living at such a speed, and the cooking part allows us some much-needed time to mentally slow down.

From the moment my sleepy eyes come into focus over my morning coffee, I'm mulling over what the first meal of the day will be. My kitchen by this point is in full-swing chaos, with my young children tearing about and the seconds ticking away before we all need to leave the house for whatever that day entails. But even if it's made in the clamour of morning chaos, breakfast should be full of different flavours and good ingredients, so you can start your day in the most energy-boosting and delicious way. This is the approach I've taken throughout the book. I've tried to give thought and care to how we cook and eat, and when and with whom, be it snacking or dining, on the move or at a more leisurely pace. I hope each chapter will offer you some joy and a few more reasons to take a break from your day to enjoy cooking your meals and savouring each mouthful.

There's still conflicting information out there about what food choices we should make and why. I believe that choosing food that makes you feel good is a reliable compass to follow.

Quite literally, go with your gut. A rainbow of fruit and veg, energy-sustaining proteins, mood-boosting nuts and seeds and wholesome carbohydrates. Processed foods make me feel awful, so I avoid them at all costs. Knowing what goes into my meals makes me feel much more balanced in energy, mood and outlook. Food can be such a game-changer.

This way of cooking and eating needn't be more expensive, laborious in preparation or boring in the taste department. If anything, quite the opposite. Cooking from scratch whenever you can actually costs a lot less, as you can batch cook, take lunch to work with you rather than buying a meal, and save any leftovers for the next day. Plus you know exactly what has gone into every meal you've eaten and can appreciate what each ingredient is doing to your body. My mum is not a fan of veering from the path of her normal eating habits, but even she has warmly welcomed all the dishes I've tested out on her from this book. I've even managed to divert her away from her classic sandwich-and-a-packet-of-crisps lunch. That is secretly very satisfying!

I've been a pescetarian since I was a small child, but I mainly eat vegetarian food. My husband occasionally eats meat, and I'm leaving it up to my kids to make up their own minds when they're old enough, so I feed them a mix of everything. As a result, most of the recipes in this book are veggie or pescatarian, but you'll also see some 'flexi' options too – these will give you some ideas of how you can introduce meat to the dish if that's what you'd prefer. My hope is that you'll play around with these meals how ever you desire to create something that's mouthwatering for you. I also had a great response to the vegan recipes in my first book, so I've included quite a few of these here too.

Aside from mealtimes, I've also included plenty of not-that-naughty treats. I am not a fan of feeling an unwanted pang of hunger during the day, so having handy, homemade, healthy snacks you can keep within reach is a huge bonus. I love to dole out dreamy treats to loved ones without telling them that they're perhaps slightly more virtuous in content than they might expect. The shock when my friends, mid-mouthful of a mountain of my Banoffee pie (page 179), hear that it is refined sugar- and dairy-free!

However you like to cook and eat, and whomever you decide to share the moment with, I hope that you delve into this book with as much glee as I had whilst creating it. That there is the 'love' bit: the positive energy that I try to power my recipes and cooking with, and I hope you will too. Let the joy of cooking and eating shine on!

MY STORE CUPBOARD

Open the doors to my kitchen cupboards and you'll find a chaotic mix of my favourite ingredients to cook with. These are the colours I use to paint my pictures – the foundations of each meal, the soul of each dish, the hearty goodness with which I fuel my body and my family's bodies.

There are no neatly labelled jars in my house; instead you'll find a wire rack of hypnotically enticing spices, a box bursting with all my favourite natural sweeteners and a shelf crammed with nuts, grains and seeds. None of these ingredients are overly expensive or difficult to find these days, but they make cooking a delicious, healthy meal that bit simpler and definitely more tantalising to the taste buds. Some of these must-haves last a long time, such as the spices, flours and oils, while others are more of a weekly purchase – but they will all boost the flavours and textures of your dishes and their all-round nutritional value.

My friends and family all have their preferred ways to eat so I love to experiment with dairy-free, sugar-free and wheat-free recipes. Many of the essentials in my cupboards offer those options, as you can substitute certain nuts or alternative flours for wheat flours, alternative milks for dairy, and honey for sugar. Once you become used to popping these on your shopping list it'll become second nature to cook and bake with them, and I guarantee they will open up new cooking horizons to you every time you step into your kitchen.

OILS AND SAUCES

COCONUT OIL

I have a love affair with coconut oil. I adore buying huge pots of the stuff and using it for everything: cooking, baking, as a make-up remover, as hand cream – you certainly get your money's worth with this magical ingredient. It melts beautifully but then solidifies again in the fridge, so it's perfect for certain bakes and is a dream to sauté with too.

OLIVE OIL

The easiest way to bring that Mediterranean goodness into your life is with olive oil. In parts of the world where olive oil is used daily, the people tend to live longer and have a lower rate of heart disease. The list of positives attached to consuming olive oil are endless. I use it to sauté, fry, in dips and as the foundation to many different dressings. It's the most versatile and tried-and-tested oil out there.

TAMARI

This rich sauce is a gluten-free version of soy sauce. It's so full of flavour and gives a salty punch to any dish. You can use it to marinate tofu, fish and chicken, and it works well in dressings too.

TAHINI

Tahini is one of my all-time favourite ingredients – so much so that I feel a slight panic when I run out of it at home. It is so very versatile and can be used in both savoury and sweet dishes. It's made from sesame seeds, so has a rich yet slightly bitter taste to it. It's very creamy and is perfect for dressings and sauces. I love to use it for baking, and of course it is the backbone of the humble hummus.

DAIRY ALTERNATIVES

ALMOND, OAT AND RICE MILKS

Dairy is fine for many people and you needn't cut it out of your diet altogether unless your body cannot tolerate it. Personally I don't include much dairy in my diet and neither does my husband, Jesse, as it doesn't seem to agree with either of us in large amounts. I adore the taste of almond milk so I use it in my morning coffee. Almond, oat and rice milks can all be found in most supermarkets these days. However, supermarket brands sometimes add sugar to their milk alternatives, so try and go for an unsweetened variety if you're not making your own from scratch. It's very easy to make your own: there are recipes for almond milk and oat milk in my first book, *Cook Happy, Cook Healthy*: they are both creamy and rich and full of flavour.

COCONUT MILK

I only started cooking with this stuff a few years ago. I'm not sure why I left it so long, as it's now one of my cupboard staples. The milk itself is great for smoothies and curries, giving them both a luxurious and slightly exotic flavour, whilst the thicker cream at the top of the tin can be used in so many ways. If you refrigerate your tins overnight then the entire contents will

solidify into coconut cream, and you can use it to make a dairy-free icing for cakes, in the creamy layer of a cheesecake or to thicken up dishes. Coconut magic at its best!

NUT BUTTERS

These can be easily homemade (see my recipe in *Cook Happy, Cook Healthy*) or bought from a shop – as long as you buy a nut butter that contains no sugar then you're on to a winner. You can buy or make almond, cashew, macadamia or any other nut butter you fancy. They're packed with protein and healthy fats to boost the health of your skin, nails, hair and heart. Use them in dressings, smoothies, or just to spread on homemade bread and crackers.

SWEET THINGS

COCONUT SUGAR

This sugar is darker in colour and richer in flavour than regular sugar, so it's a dream to bake with. Coconut palm sugar has not been refined, so you get the sweetness and flavour without the horrific saccharine rollercoaster that ensues after you gorge on the white stuff. Although it is lower on the glycemic index, it should still be regarded as a treat and not eaten in excessive amounts. Most of the sweet treats in this book are pretty low in even natural sugars, bar the odd cheeky cake found in Baked Goodies.

HONEY

Thank you, lovely bees, for producing the most incredible natural sweetness. Honey can be so healing and has been used as a natural medicine for thousands of years. It works very well in bakes, sauces and dressings, and brings life to so many dishes in this book.

MAPLE SYRUP

Maple syrup comes from the sap of the maple tree, and is a nice way to sweeten bakes and sauces due to its rich flavour. It's an unrefined sugar, so is a popular swap for traditional white sugar. It is more expensive than buying sugar, but you don't need to use too much as it's very sweet naturally.

RAW CACAO

Raw cacao is a dream. I've become so used to using it in recipes or for making my own chocolate that I now prefer its bitter, rich flavour to shop-bought choc. It's the most natural form of the cocoa bean and is full of antioxidants, which aid your health in so many ways. It is also a great mood-booster, as it raises the level of serotonin in the brain (this is often my justification when I simply must have chocolate after dinner). It's great for bakes and can be easily sweetened by using a little honey.

FLOURS AND GRAINS

BUCKWHEAT

I'm quite new to buckwheat but I really love its flavour and versatility. Although it's confusingly called buck*wheat* there is actually no wheat in this superfood. In fact, it's collected from a seed-bearing flower and is related to the rhubarb. It's slightly nutty in flavour and can be used as a porridge alternative. It can also be ground into a flour, which is brilliant for baking.

SPELT FLOUR

You'll see that many recipes in this book use spelt flour. I really enjoy using it and love how it tastes; I find it has more depth and flavour than regular flour. It also has a lower gluten-content, so it's useful for those who find gluten doesn't always agree with them (it does still contain gluten, however, so it's not suitable if you're coeliac or gluten-intolerant).

RICE FLOUR

Rice flour is gluten-free and is really nice to use for baking. It does make your bakes slightly more crumbly though, so some modifications need to be made when adapting a cake recipe to include it. It's great for pancakes, biscuits, cakes and as a coating in certain savoury dishes.

QUINOA

Despite having existed for thousands of years in South America, a few years ago many of us in the UK might have thought quinoa was the name of a new *Star Wars* character. Fast-forward half a decade and most of us are well aware of this superfood. It's readily available in most supermarkets and is inexpensive. It is a great alternative to rice and pasta and is brilliant for beefing up soups and salads. I'm sneaking it into this section since it isn't actually a grain – it's a pseudocereal, so it's gluten-free and is full of protein and fibre.

RICE AND PASTA

My kids love rice and pasta, so I always find them to be good staples for a family meal since everyone will eat it. You'll find recipes using both in this book that are easy and freshly made to boost your diet with homemade goodness. When you can, try and buy brown rice and pasta. Most supermarkets will offer this option, and these days many shops or online stores have various pastas, from spelt to quinoa-based to wholegrain. White pasta and rice have been through a refining process, during which they lose their nutrients and natural colour. Brown rice and pasta will be much kinder to your gut, and I think they taste way better too.

DRIED FRUITS AND SEEDS

DATES

Dates are a juicy sweet treat that I love to use in baking and smoothies, and also just chomp whole. They're so naturally sweet and gooey, so are great for making energy balls. Most of you will also be aware of how good they are for your gut. They keep you regular and promote a healthy digestive system and heart.

UNSULPHURED APRICOTS

These little beauts are black in colour so look less attractive than their bright orange cousins. Their colour is due to the fact that they have not had sulphur added to them during the drying process. This means they keep their delicious rich flavour. Great for energy balls, cakes, biscuits and flapjacks.

CHIA SEEDS

These tiny South American wonders might not look like much, but they're packed with fibre, protein and vitamins. They can be thrown into smoothies, salads and soups, and can also be used instead of egg in some recipes, as they become gelatinous. The seeds expand in liquid so they can be made into gorgeous little puddings, perfect as a sweet breakfast treat.

GOJI BERRIES

These gems are bright red and are deliciously sweet yet slightly tart. They're full of antioxidants, fibre and vitamin C. They add a chewy fruitiness to bakes and can liven up a savoury meal in the same way.

Breakfast, you wonderful sunrise celebration! I'm so glad you exist to ease me into a new day by reviving my sleepy body and mind. All of us will gravitate towards one particular meal of the day and will tend to see the others as less pertinent to our overall health and wellbeing. For me, breakfast is non-negotiable. Without it I will most definitely be a grumpy old sardine with a severe lack of focus and humour towards what lies ahead. But give me a hearty primary meal and I'm good to go!

From that first smell of coffee, after my little dawn raiders have broken the silence in our house, I'm strategising how breakfast might take shape. How I start my day usually sets the trend for the next twelve or so hours, so I want to get it right. On weekdays time is tight in our house, as each member of the family races to the day's starting line. This is when the kitchen is usually at its noisiest, as discussions spark, food orders come rolling in from the kids and my husband, and I scurry around getting mouths fed and bodies fuelled, my own included. Quick, fresh and flavoursome meals need to be whipped up and dished out quickly. I'm massively on board with a flavoured porridge of late; I'm a fan of a warm and hearty bowl of regular porridge, but it can get a bit samey in the winter months.

Adding a dash of drama, flavourwise, keeps me on track, and the Carrot cake porridge on page 15 is one of my favourite kick-starts for the morning. If you're into smoothies you can whizz up and dash out the door with, you should find the ones in this chapter tasty and very filling too. Packed with vitamins, proteins and carbs to give you energy and enthusiasm for the day ahead.

At the weekend I love to stretch breakfast into a marathon eating session. The pace is slower as there is usually no need to rush against an ominous ticking clock. My dressing gown stays on, my hair remains chaotically scrambled in a bun, and I cook and eat on repeat. The Fruity breakfast omelette on page 33 allows me to satisfy my sweet tooth whilst appeasing my body's need for sustaining protein. It's my new weekend classic.

I always find that if I've had a delicious and nutritious breakfast then my energy until bedtime is much more balanced and my mood less frenetic and stuck in yesterday. A new day means a new menu and new possibilities.

BREAKFAST

APRICOT BUCKWHEAT PORRIDGE

SERVES 4

Buckwheat and I only became acquainted quite recently, but my goodness do we get on. Despite its name, buckwheat contains zero wheat, so for those of you who can't handle gluten this oat alternative is perfect. It has a slightly nuttier taste, which gives this breakfast dish a rich and wholesome flavour. The apricots add sweetness and even more fibre, making this one hell of a nutritious and delicious way to start your day! It's quick and easy, and a nice twist on a warm bowl of porridge on a cold day. Cook it up and get that fire in your belly for a busy day ahead!

180g buckwheat groats

575ml milk (almond, rice or dairy)

4 unsulphured dried apricots, plus extra to serve

¾ tsp ground nutmeg, plus extra to serve

2 tsp coconut oil

2 tbsp sunflower seeds, to serve

Cover the buckwheat groats in double their quantity of water and leave to soak overnight or for at least 6 hours.

Once the buckwheat has soaked, drain and rinse very well under running water.

Place the rinsed buckwheat, milk, dried apricots and ground nutmeg in a pan (with a lid) and set over a medium heat. Bring to a simmer, put the lid on and cook for 12–15 minutes, stirring every now and then, until the buckwheat has absorbed most of the liquid and is thick.

Add the porridge to an upright blender (or use a stick blender), together with the coconut oil, and process for a minute or two until smooth. If you like it a little thinner, add in another 1–2 tablespoons of milk or water.

Serve immediately in bowls with some extra chopped dried apricot, ground nutmeg and sunflower seeds scattered over.

CARROT CAKE PORRIDGE

SERVES 4

I adore carrot cake and love breakfast, so combining the two was only natural. This warming bowl will awaken your taste buds with its zing and spice and give you oodles of energy to begin your day. The juicy raisins add sweetness and fibre, and the oats will give off that slow-release energy you need to see you through your morning. Plus, the carrot adds more veg to your day, which is never a bad thing! If you start off with a good dose of brightly coloured veg, you're already on to a winner. Although this breakfast dish tastes decadent and luxurious it is time-sparing and easy, leaving you plenty of time for everything else that clutters your morning.

180g rolled porridge oats

270ml almond milk or rice milk

Small handful of raisins

1 tsp ground cinnamon or ½ tsp mixed spice, plus extra to serve

1 carrot, peeled and coarsely grated

Grated zest of 1 orange

2 tbsp pumpkin seeds, to serve

Put the oats, milk, raisins and cinnamon (or mixed spice) into a pan with 550ml of water and set over a medium–low heat. Simmer gently for 10–15 minutes, stirring now and again, until the porridge is thick and creamy.

Stir in most of the carrot and orange zest. Serve in bowls with the remaining carrot, zest and pumpkin seeds scattered on top.

STRAWBERRIES & CREAM PORRIDGE

SERVES 4

The marriage of strawberries and cream evokes instant images of warm summer air and bright shining mornings. That very image inspired this breakfast – even though porridge can be seen as more of a wintery start to the day. Cashew cream is dairy-free and adds a delightful creamy texture and light taste to the porridge. The mint lifts all of the flavours with its crisp freshness and brings this recipe together so well. This is a quick and easy breakfast but revives a tired bowl of oats in minutes. Summer bliss.

180g rolled porridge oats

270ml almond milk or rice milk

200g strawberries, hulled, plus extra to serve

1 tsp honey

2 tbsp cashew cream or coconut cream

A few fresh mint leaves, to serve

Put the oats and milk in a pan with 550ml of water and set over a medium–low heat. Simmer gently for 10–15 minutes, stirring now and again, until the porridge is thick and creamy. Meanwhile, mash the strawberries to a pulp with a fork and stir in the honey.

Serve the porridge in bowls. Swirl in the muddled strawberries and a little cashew cream or coconut cream. Top with a few more strawberries and scatter over the mint leaves.

CARROT CAKE
PORRIDGE p15

APRICOT
BUCKWHEAT
PORRIDGE p14

STRAWBERRIES
& CREAM
PORRIDGE p15

BUCKWHEAT CREPES

WITH BLUEBERRY, BANANA & COCONUT CREAM

MAKES 10 PANCAKES

Buckwheat flour is such a lovely ingredient: it's light, slightly nutty and gluten-free. Buckwheat deceptively contains no wheat at all, and in fact derives from the seeds of a flowering plant. It makes these crepes light and easy on the gut and full of flavour. We adore crepes in our house and all have our preferred ways to devour them: I love to pile mine high with fruit and coconut cream. Knock yourself out!

160g white spelt flour
40g buckwheat flour
1 tsp baking powder
4 eggs
400ml milk (almond, rice or dairy)
Coconut oil, for frying
125g blueberries, to serve
125g strawberries, hulled and sliced, to serve
2 ripe bananas, peeled and sliced, to serve
150g coconut cream, to serve
Maple syrup or honey, for drizzling
Pinch of fine sea salt

Sieve the flours, baking powder and salt into a large mixing bowl. In a separate bowl, whisk together the eggs and milk. Make a well in the centre of the flour and slowly pour in the liquid mixture, mixing all the time until you have a smooth batter. Leave the batter to rest for 15 minutes.

When ready to cook, heat a little coconut oil in a 20cm non-stick pan until hot. Stir the batter and pour a small ladleful into the pan, swirling it so the mixture spreads out to the edges. Cook for about a minute until the top of the pancake begins to bubble, then flip the pancake over and cook until dry and golden. Remove from the pan and keep covered in a low oven while you continue with the remaining batter.

Serve the crepes with the berries, bananas and coconut cream, with maple syrup or honey drizzled over.

ROSEMARY AND DATE SPELT LOAF

MAKES 1 LOAF

The Spelt and goji berry loaf in Cook Happy, Cook Healthy *got a lot of love from quite a few of you, so I set to work finding another variation that would impress you just as much for this book. The smell of rosemary is very comforting and works so well with the sweet dates. Your taste buds can't work out if a slice of this bread is a sweet or savoury treat, as the flavours layer up and jump out individually. This bake requires no kneading, so it's quick and easy as well as delicious.*

500g wholegrain spelt flour

1 tsp baking powder

1 tsp bicarbonate of soda

2 tsp finely chopped fresh rosemary leaves

60g dates, pitted and chopped

1 tbsp maple syrup or honey

530ml tepid water

1 tsp sea salt

Preheat the oven to 200°C/180°C fan/400°F/Gas mark 6. Lightly grease a 1kg loaf tin and line it with baking parchment.

Thoroughly mix all the dry ingredients together in a bowl, then add the honey and water and mix again until just combined.

Pour into the loaf tin and bake in the oven for 50 minutes, then carefully remove the loaf from its tin and continue to bake for a further 10 minutes (this gives it a better crust).

Remove the loaf from the oven and leave to cool completely before cutting, otherwise all the steam will escape, resulting in a drier loaf. Once cool, cut into slices and enjoy with a little butter or coconut oil.

PEACH BREAKFAST CRUMBLE

SERVES 4

I remember clearly going to a mate's house for dinner when I was about eighteen and her mum serving up baked peaches and honey for dessert. Having only ever experienced the choc-ice post-dinner at home, this seemed novel and quite exotic. I now love to bake peaches whenever possible and breakfast seems like a pretty good place to start. I love this recipe for three reasons: first, it makes your house smell like a fairy tale; second, the crumble tastes like heaven and warms your belly nicely; and third, it's a great way to get some fibrous fruit into your diet right at the start of the day. These work well at weekends as they take a while to bake – but boy, is it worth the wait.

60g extra virgin coconut oil

80g white spelt flour

70g rolled oats

60g coconut palm sugar

½ tsp ground cinnamon

2 tbsp chia seeds

2 tbsp pumpkin seeds

6 ripe peaches or nectarines, halved and stones removed

Yoghurt (Greek, soy or coconut), to serve

1 tbsp fresh mint leaves, to serve

Pinch of sea salt

Preheat the oven to 200°C/180°C fan/400°F/Gas mark 6.

In a large bowl, rub the coconut oil into the flour until you have gravel-sized lumps. Mix in the oats, coconut palm sugar, cinnamon, chia and pumpkin seeds and a pinch of salt. Set aside.

Place the peach halves on a baking tray and top with the crumble mixture. Bake in the oven for 25–30 minutes until golden and the peaches are soft. Serve with yoghurt and a few mint leaves.

COCOA, CHIA, KALE & OAT BREAKFAST SMOOTHIE

SERVES 2

This smoothie is a household favourite. My husband and I love it as it tastes heavenly and we know we are boosting our morning with friendly green kale – and my kids think it's a chocolaty treat and glug it down without the slightest knowledge of the hidden green stuff! Win-win. The chia seeds add some omega to your day and the oats and banana give you plenty of energy to boost your morning. If I end up with leftover smoothie in the blender, I pour it into ice lolly moulds and freeze it for the kids for later. It's one of the most frequently made recipes in this book in the Wood house, and hopefully it will be in yours too!

1 ripe banana, sliced and frozen

50g oats

100g kale, rinsed and dried, and tough stems removed

1 tbsp chia seeds

3 dates, pitted

1 tbsp unsweetened cocoa powder

350ml oat milk

1 tsp vanilla extract

Ice, to serve

Put the frozen banana slices, oats, kale, chia seeds, dates and cocoa powder in the bowl of a food processor or in a high-speed blender and blitz until ground down. Add in the milk and vanilla extract and blitz for another minute or two until smooth.

Pour into two large glasses with ice and serve immediately.

STRAWBERRY, AVOCADO & HEMP SMOOTHIE

SERVES 2

For those who don't like eating first thing, or who simply can't find the time, this meal in a glass is the perfect solution. The avocado gives the smoothie the most luxurious creaminess as well as a delicious dose of good fats that will help your skin glow and your body thrive. Hemp is also extremely beneficial – it is a great source of protein and omegas 3 and 6. This is not just an easy-to-make smoothie: you can also drizzle it on top of salads or porridge.

400g strawberries, hulled and frozen

1 ripe avocado, peeled and stone removed

4 tbsp shelled hemp seeds

350ml milk (almond, rice or dairy)

1 tsp vanilla extract

Put the frozen strawberries in the bowl of a food processor or in a high-speed blender and blitz until ground down. Add the rest of the ingredients and blitz for a minute or two until completely smooth.

Pour into two large glasses and serve immediately.

FROZEN LATTE

SERVES 4

My lists of loves goes a little like this: my family, my friends, COFFEE. My husband is the same, so much of our time is spent looking forward to ceremonial hiatuses when we can drink coffee and take a few moments out of our busy days. This morning mix-up gives your coffee fix a cool, refreshing twist and is perfect for summertime. The bananas add extra creaminess and the walnuts add a roasted flavour which I adore.

1 ripe banana, peeled, sliced and frozen

40g walnuts

240ml almond milk

40ml freshly brewed coffee

1 tsp maple syrup or honey

Cocoa powder or ground cinnamon, for dusting (optional)

Ice, to serve

Put the frozen banana slices and walnuts in the bowl of a food processor and blitz for a minute or two until they have ground down into a paste.

With the motor still running, pour in the almond milk, coffee and maple syrup or honey until the mixture is thoroughly combined. Pour into a glass with some ice, dust with cocoa powder or ground cinnamon (if using) and serve immediately.

MULTI-SEED BREAKFAST BARS TO GO

MAKES 8-10
BREAKFAST BARS

These bars of goodness can be whipped up quickly and stored for a busy week. Grab one on your way out the door, pack one in your bag for a breakfast on the run or enjoy snacking on them throughout the day. They are light and crisp but still chewy and moreish without containing any dairy or refined sugars. They are likely to be so much better for you than the pre-made, shop-bought equivalent and taste way more delicious than anything in a packet.

165g oats
100g puffed rice
40g sunflower seeds
40g pumpkin seeds
40g chia seeds
40g desiccated coconut
60g unsulphured dried
apricots, chopped
100g almond butter
150g brown rice syrup
60g coconut oil
Pinch of sea salt

*Cashew and white chocolate drizzle
(optional)*
100g cashew nuts, soaked
2 tbsp coconut oil, melted
5 tbsp rice or oat milk
3 tbsp honey

Line a 28 x 20cm cake tin with baking parchment.

Put the oats, puffed rice, sunflower, pumpkin and chia seeds, desiccated coconut, dried apricots and a pinch of salt into a bowl and combine.

Put the almond butter, rice syrup and coconut oil in a pan and set over a medium heat. Stir constantly until the coconut oil is melted and the mixture has come together. Pour this into the dry mixture and thoroughly combine, ensuring the oats and seeds are completely coated in the wet mixture.

Spread the mixture in the lined tin and compact into place with the back of a spoon. Leave to cool, then cover and refrigerate for at least 1 hour or until well chilled (this makes it easier to slice).

For the drizzle, drain the cashew nuts, add to a food processor or high speed blender and blitz until smooth. Add the coconut oil, rice milk and honey and combine.

When ready to eat, slice up the breakfast bars into squares or rectangles and gently remove from the tray. Drizzle over the cashew white chocolate and serve immediately, or store in an airtight container in the fridge for up to a week.

COURGETTE & SWEET POTATO HASH

WITH EGGS

SERVES 4

I love dishes like this one. These sorts of recipes usually begin with me raiding my fridge for leftovers and then cooking them up in the tastiest possible way. We always have sweet potato in the house as it's my daughter's favourite, so naturally it's become the foundation of many recipes. Sweet potatoes hold so much goodness and give you steady energy for your day ahead. This is the perfect recipe if you fancy holding a CoppaFeel! boob brunch. I'm a patron of CoppaFeel! (the breast cancer awareness charity) and I love this idea as brunch and boobs should go hand in hand. If you want to know how you can set up your own, head to the website coppafeel.org.

450g sweet potato, cut into small cubes (no need to peel)

3½ tbsp olive oil

2 courgettes, diced

1 red onion, diced

2 cloves garlic, crushed

4 eggs

Small handful of fresh flat-leaf parsley leaves, roughly chopped

Dried chilli flakes, to serve (optional)

Sea salt and freshly ground black pepper

Cook the sweet potato in a pan of boiling water for exactly 4 minutes. Drain well.

Put 3 tablespoons of the oil in a pan and place over a medium heat. Add the sweet potato and cook for 5 minutes, until golden. Add the courgettes, onion and garlic, and sauté for another 5 minutes until everything is cooked through and golden. Season to taste with salt and pepper.

Heat the remaining half tablespoon of oil in a separate pan and fry the eggs to your liking. Plate up the sweet potato and courgette hash with an egg on top and the parsley and chilli (if using) scattered over. Serve immediately.

FLEXI OPTION

Add in 100g diced chorizo when you throw in the courgette and onion. It will add texture and a smoky flavour to your eggs.

SCRAMBLED EGGS

WITH SPINACH, RED PEPPER & RADISH

SERVES 4

Eggs. Quick, easy and very nutritious, yet they can get boring. I get into habits when I cook eggs, and I can forget how jazzy they can be when a little thought goes into the process. This dish is so quick to make but packs a punch, with spinach for a green boost and magical, anti-imflammatory turmeric. The coconut cream gives a luxurious texture to this dish, and I love to add goat's cheese for even more flavour and decadence. A glorious way to begin your day!

150g spinach leaves

Extra virgin olive oil, for drizzling

5 eggs

120ml coconut cream or regular cream

¼ tsp ground turmeric

100g roasted red peppers from a jar, sliced

4 radishes, thinly sliced

4 slices rye bread, or gluten-free if you prefer

1 clove garlic, peeled

60g soft goat's cheese (optional)

Sea salt and freshly ground black pepper

Heat a dry pan over a high heat. Add the spinach and sprinkle over a few drops of water. Stir the spinach until it has wilted down completely. Remove to a sieve and gently press out any excess water. Return to the pan and season with a little salt, pepper and a drizzling of extra virgin olive oil.

Break the eggs into a bowl and whisk together with the cream and turmeric. Season with half a teaspoon of salt and a good grinding of pepper.

Add the egg mixture, red peppers and most of the radish to the spinach and set over a medium heat. With a spatula, continuously move the spinach and egg mixture around as it cooks. Just before you think it is ready, when it still seems a little too wet, turn off the heat.

Toast the bread, scrape the garlic clove across the surface, then drizzle with a little extra virgin olive oil and a very small pinch of sea salt. Pile the egg mixture on top and scatter over the remaining sliced radish and the goat's cheese (if using). Finish off with another drizzling of extra virgin olive oil.

FRUITY BREAKFAST OMELETTE

MAKES 2 OMELETTES

I have a very sweet tooth, so any opportunity to make a meal sweet I will. This sweet omelette is essentially a pancake without the flour. It's light and fluffy yet is a huge hit of protein which will give you boundless energy throughout the morning. The fruit offers some wonderful vitamins and nutrients and boosts this dish's sweet, heavenly flavour. I love to cook this at weekends and enjoy it whilst the kids are creating chaos nearby.

1 very ripe banana, peeled and mashed

½ tsp ground cinnamon, plus extra for dusting

4 eggs

60g blueberries, plus extra to serve

1 tbsp coconut oil

1 tbsp maple syrup or honey

1 tbsp almond butter

In a large bowl mix together the banana and cinnamon. Beat in the eggs until thoroughly combined, then stir in the blueberries.

Put half the coconut oil in a non-stick pan and place over a medium–low heat. Once the coconut oil is hot, but not smoking, add half the egg mixture and spread out to cover the base of the pan. As the egg begins to set, drag the sides of the omelette towards the centre of the pan and allow the raw egg to fill in any gaps.

When the egg is completely cooked through, fold it in half and slide it on to a plate. Repeat with the remaining egg mixture.

To serve, combine the maple syrup or honey and almond butter and drizzle over the pancakes. Top with more blueberries and a dusting of cinnamon.

Although Great Britain is drenched in rain for 85 per cent of the year (or at least that's what it feels like), our little country has some absolute jewels: incredible historic buildings, the NHS, pubs, Mel and Sue, and . . . elevenses.

Why wait until lunch when you really don't have to? An hour or so after breakfast my belly starts to feel empty again, which signals to my brain to start mulling over what I might consume next. Food-obsessed? YES!

Just a little nibble, something to keep my blood sugar levels up and my spirits high. Snacking is one of life's pleasures, but it doesn't have to mean processed, sugar-laden gut bloaters. Choose your snacks wisely and they'll simply pep you up until your next meal. Make them from scratch and you're laughing! You'll know just what's gone into them and how they are helping your body.

In this chapter you'll find many wonderful meal-inbetweeners, which you can make quickly and pack in your bag if you're out and about. I love to serve many of these little snacks when I have friends over at the weekend too. A cup of tea goes hand in hand with something sweet to nibble on, like the Blueberry & banana muffins on page 42 (my kids adore helping me make and eat them too). It's very much a given that any guest will be offered some form of cake or snack approximately twenty-five seconds after walking into my house. It feels almost awkward if this transaction doesn't take place.

If sweet treats aren't your sort of thing and it's savoury you crave, I hope you enjoy my twists on hummus: Balsamic & red pepper hummus and Oil-free hummus & veg sticks, both on page 49. I love hummus, and my kids eat it by the spoonful and want it on everything. It's quick and easy yet still an impressive snack to whip up.

If you're not a fan of breakfast and prefer a slightly later start time for your digestive system to kick into gear, then this chapter will offer ideas for your mid-morning munch. Batch-make the Almond, chia & goji flapjacks (page 39) and store them away until hunger hits, or take one along for your day at work. SO much tastier, cheaper and healthier than buying a shop-bought version, which has spoonfuls of refined sugar in its buttery base.

I will always love snacking as I'm not a fan of feeling insanely hungry (who is?!). I start to get cranky and low-energy, which no one around me should experience regularly. This is where the wonder of elevenses comes into play. A small bite to tide me over as my day flies along. These mini dishes are all family-friendly, and make life that bit easier when a busy morning depletes your energy levels.

Tick-tock – hurry up 11 a.m., I say.

ELEVENSES

GINGER & LEMON LOAF CAKE

SERVES 8-10

My most used and loved cookbook is Nigella Lawson's How to Be a Domestic Goddess. *Some pages are so smeared with cake mix I can barely read the words anymore. It's heavenly, decadent and soooo Nigella. Hence the adoration. One of my favourite cakes from this book, which spins me back to childhood, is her ginger cake with lemon icing. Something about these two flavours together makes me weak at the knees. This version of that cake uses much less sugar from a combination of natural sugars. The blackstrap molasses is high in calcium, magnesium and iron and gives this cake a rich flavour. Although this cake is made up of natural goodness it is still a treat, so don't eat the whole thing in one go! Enjoy a slab of this with a cup of Soothing ginger and turmeric tea (page 120).*

125g coconut oil or unsalted butter

100g coconut palm sugar

100g maple syrup or honey

100g blackstrap molasses

60g root ginger, peeled and very finely grated

1 tsp ground cinnamon

150ml milk (almond, rice or dairy)

2 eggs, beaten

¾ tsp bicarbonate of soda

300g white spelt flour

For the icing:

200g cream cheese, or dairy-free alternative

Grated zest of 2 lemons, plus extra for scattering

1 tbsp set honey

Preheat the oven to 180°C/160°C fan/350°F/Gas mark 4. Grease a 20 x 10cm loaf tin and line with baking parchment.

Put the coconut oil or butter, coconut palm sugar, maple syrup or honey, molasses, ginger and cinnamon in a pan and set over a medium heat until the sugar has dissolved.

Remove from the heat and whisk in the milk, eggs, bicarbonate of soda and flour until thoroughly combined.

Transfer the mixture to the lined loaf tin and bake for 45–55 minutes, until a skewer inserted into the centre of the cake comes out mostly clean, as you want it to be a little moist. If the top is browning too quickly, cover with foil. Remove from the oven and cool in the tin for 10 minutes, then transfer to a wire rack to cool completely.

Meanwhile, combine the cream cheese, lemon zest and honey and keep in the fridge. Once the cake is completely cool, spread the icing on top and scatter over a little more lemon zest.

ALMOND, CHIA & GOJI FLAPJACKS

MAKES 10-12 FLAPJACKS

Shop-bought flapjacks are notoriously packed with refined sugar and oodles of butter, and often contain very little goodness to sustain your energy throughout the day. These ones tell a very different story – still crammed with flavour yet without any refined sugar. They're so easy to make and fun to whip up with the kids, as there's very little that can go wrong with these treats. They're family-friendly and great to have stored in an airtight tin for whenever you need an energy pick-me-up!

140g coconut oil or unsalted butter
60g coconut palm sugar
4 tbsp honey or maple syrup
250g jumbo oats
Large handful of flaked almonds
2 tbsp chia seeds
2 tbsp goji berries

Preheat the oven to 190°C/170°C fan/375°F/Gas mark 5 and line a 24 x 16cm tray bake tin with baking parchment.

Put the coconut oil or butter, sugar and honey or maple syrup in a pan and place over a low–medium heat. Simmer gently, stirring regularly, until the sugar has dissolved and the mixture has come together.

Remove from the heat and stir in the remaining ingredients until well combined. Transfer to the lined tin and press down very firmly to compact the mixture. Bake in the oven for 16–20 minutes until golden.

Remove the tin from the oven, and with the back of a spoon, gently press down on the flapjack mixture. While it's still hot, gently cut the mixture into squares, then leave in the tin to cool completely.

Once cool, you can store in an airtight container for up to a week.

GUACAMOLE CRACKER SNACKS

SERVES 2

Crackers are my most-eaten snack. I love to spread them with nut butters, honey or butter for a yummy, energising and quick bite to eat. These light and healthy crackers are easy to whip up and work well with the homemade guacamole, which is so creamy thanks to the tahini. They can then be topped with anything you like; I love sun-dried tomatoes and olives for a flavoursome nutritious snack.

For the crackers:

100g white spelt flour, plus extra for dusting

½ tsp baking powder

30g unsalted butter or coconut oil, chilled and cut into cubes

Sea salt

For the guacamole:

1 large ripe avocado, peeled and stone removed

1 tbsp lime juice

1 tbsp tahini

2 tsp extra virgin olive oil, plus extra for drizzling

1 small clove garlic, crushed

Sea salt and freshly ground black pepper

Topping suggestions:

Sun-dried tomatoes

Olives

Pumpkin seeds

Parsley, chopped

Soft-boiled egg

Dried chilli flakes

Preheat the oven to 180°C/160°C fan/350°F/Gas mark 4 and line a baking sheet with baking parchment.

To make the crackers, put the flour, baking powder, chilled butter (or coconut oil) and a large pinch of sea salt in the bowl of a food processor and blitz until you have fine breadcrumbs. Add 2 tablespoons of water and pulse on and off until it comes together in a ball of dough. If the dough is still crumbly add a few drops of water at a time until it forms a smooth ball.

Roll out the dough as thinly as possible on a lightly floured surface, dusting with more flour as you go to prevent sticking. Brush the dough with a little water and sprinkle over a little more salt. Cut the dough into odd shapes – squares and rectangles, or anything you like. Transfer to the lined baking sheet and bake for 12–14 minutes until dry and biscuity. Remove from the oven and transfer to a wire rack to cool completely. Store in an airtight container for up to 4 days.

To make the guacamole, blitz the avocado in a food processor with the lime juice, tahini, olive oil and garlic until completely smooth. Season to taste and transfer to a bowl.

Spread on to the crackers and top with any of the topping suggestions, or anything else you like. Drizzle with a little olive oil and serve immediately.

BLUEBERRY & BANANA MUFFINS

MAKES 6 MUFFINS

We go through so many bananas in our house. A bunch lasts about three days as they're munched on as snacks, used to beef up smoothies and, more often than not, used in bakes. My kids love these muffins and like to help me make them too. They're packed with juicy bursting blueberries, which offer a good dose of vitamins, and have no refined sugar or dairy, so are perfect if you or your family have an intolerance. They're light and fluffy and make the perfect mid-morning snack!

100g rice flour or white spelt flour
80g ground almonds
½ tsp bicarbonate of soda
½ tsp baking powder
1 very ripe banana, peeled and mashed
1 tsp vanilla extract
120ml rice milk
100ml maple syrup or honey
150g blueberries
Pinch of sea salt

Preheat the oven to 200°C/180°C fan/400°F/Gas mark 6 and line a muffin tray with paper cases.

Combine the flour, ground almonds, bicarbonate of soda, baking powder and a pinch of salt in a large bowl.

In a separate bowl combine the banana, vanilla extract, milk, maple syrup or honey and blueberries. Add this to the flour mixture and stir to combine.

Divide the mixture evenly between the 6 muffin cases. Bake for 20–25 minutes, or until a skewer inserted into the middle of a muffin comes out clean. Remove from the oven and leave to cool on a wire rack.

CINNAMON APPLE BALLS

MAKES 18-20 BALLS

My husband used to buy a shop-bought version of these energy balls so I was determined to work out how to recreate the taste in a more natural and cost-effective way. After a bit of experimenting I'm more than happy with the flavour and texture of these little mid-morning treats. They're sweet, so you can feel a little naughty, but they also have fibre from the fruit, protein from the nuts and omega from the chia seeds. Cinnamon is also a great natural way to lower your blood sugar.

120g dried soft apple rings, or unsulphured dried apricots

2 tbsp chia seeds, plus extra for coating (optional)

1 tbsp coconut oil, melted

2 tsp ground cinnamon

3 Medjool dates, pitted

2 tbsp apple juice

10 walnuts

Place all the ingredients in the bowl of a food processor and blitz until they come together when pressed between your fingers.

Shape the mixture into little balls, roughly one heaped teaspoon per ball, then refrigerate for 30 minutes to firm up. If you like, you can coat the balls in chia seeds. Store in an airtight container in the fridge for up to 2 weeks.

AVOCADO CREAM

WITH CHARGRILLED CUCUMBER

SERVES 2

One summer in Ibiza a friend of ours cooked us up a big, beautiful dinner using local ingredients. The meal that he served up was unusual and delicious, so I went about trying to recreate it as soon as I got home to England. I had never even thought about charring cucumber before I had this dish, but now it's become one of my fave ways to eat it. Cucumbers can be terribly boring and are reduced to a sandwich filler at the best of times. This dish brings life to the humble cucumber and works perfectly with the creamy avocado. This is a great starter if you have mates over for dinner and is also perfect as a little mid-morning snack.

1 large ripe avocado, peeled and stone removed

1 tsp lemon juice

1 tbsp tahini

1 tbsp extra virgin olive oil, plus more for drizzling

1 small clove garlic, crushed

½ cucumber

2 tsp olive oil

2 slices of sourdough or gluten-free bread, or 2 rice cakes

1 tbsp fresh flat-leaf parsley leaves, chopped

Sea salt and freshy ground black pepper

In a bowl mash the avocado with a fork. Mix in the lemon juice, tahini, extra virgin olive oil and garlic until combined. Season to taste with salt and pepper, cover and set to one side.

Place a grill pan over a high heat. Halve the cucumber lengthways and cut into bite-size chunks. Toss with the olive oil and season with salt and pepper. Once the grill pan is very hot, add the cucumber and fry for 2–3 minutes on each side until golden and charred.

Toast the bread or plate up your rice cakes, drizzle with a little extra virgin olive oil, top with the avocado and cucumber and scatter over the parsley. Serve immediately.

BALSAMIC & RED PEPPER HUMMUS

SERVES 2-4 AS A SNACK

400g tin chickpeas
80ml tahini
Juice of ½ lemon
1 clove garlic, crushed
1 tbsp balsamic vinegar, plus extra for drizzling
100g roasted red peppers from a jar
3 tbsp extra virgin olive oil, plus extra for drizzling
¼ tsp smoked paprika
50g feta (optional)
Spelt bread, to serve
Sea salt and freshly ground black pepper

Hummus is one of my all-time faves, so I'm constantly thinking up ways to put a new spin on its flavour and texture. One of my stepson's friends mentioned his dad does a fantastic balsamic hummus, so I instantly pinched the idea and ran with it! This is the king of hummuses with its kick of balsamic and extra-juicy toppings. I could eat the whole lot in one sitting. Smear it over toast, dip crudités in it, or dollop it on the side of your plate at mealtimes.

Drain and rinse the chickpeas, then place in the bowl of a food processor along with the tahini, lemon juice, garlic, balsamic vinegar, red peppers, extra-virgin olive oil and 3 tablespoons of water. Purée until smooth and creamy. Season to taste with salt and pepper, and add a little more olive oil and lemon juice if needed.

Serve in a bowl, topped with the paprika and feta (if using) and drizzle with balsamic vinegar and olive oil, with the bread alongside.

OIL-FREE HUMMUS & VEG STICKS

SERVES 3-4 AS A SNACK

400g tin chickpeas
5 tbsp yoghurt (Greek, soy or coconut)
1 clove garlic, crushed
1 tbsp cashew butter
Vegetable of your choice, such as carrot, cucumber, celery, pepper
1 apple
¼ tsp of sea salt

My mission to try out every possible hummus recipe continues: we're now in the realms of yogurt and cashew butter. This hummus is so light and creamy and has a nutty kick from the cashews. Use any sort of yoghurt you prefer. My personal favourite is soya, as it makes the hummus almost sweet and works so well when you dip apples and carrots into its thick consistency. A dreamy snack when lunch feels a long way off!

Drain and rinse the chickpeas. Add to the bowl of a food processor with the yoghurt, garlic and cashew butter and blitz until thoroughly combined. Add a little water if you find it too thick.

Slice your chosen vegetables into matchsticks and serve alongside the hummus.

I have always been a lover of soup and its cooler sister, salad.

Soup is a wonderful way to get through the winter months, feeding your torso with warmth and drenching your tired body with vitamins. It's the most comforting of all dishes and can be quickly made with great ease. You may wonder what the point is of making soup from scratch when it is so easily bought. Well, in this chapter you'll find some very quick and easy soup recipes that will taste so much more full-bodied and divine than tinned soup from your local supermarket. You'll know how much salt has gone into it and that there are no hidden sugars. It's all 100 per cent natural goodness. When my husband is away on tour with his band I become a soup-eating, PJ-wearing sloth every night at home. I put the babies to bed, whip up a delicious soup and enjoy every moment of its internal hug. It's so quick and simple, and I can save some for the next day for my daughter, Honey, who is also a soup enthusiast. It's a great way to get veg into your kids. Having said that, my son Rex is yet to be won over by soup, as his suspicious eye telescopically picks out every possible vegetable that could be lurking within! Luckily I have some other sneaky tricks for Rex when it comes to vegetables (for example, check out the Chocolate milk on page 113). Honey, on the other hand, will dip bread into any soup like it's

going out of fashion. One out of two ain't bad!

Soup doesn't have to be restricted to the winter months of course. The Veggie Vietnamese soup on page 52 is the perfect fresh and crunchy soup that is divine on a summer evening. It's packed with flavour and punch, yet is so subtle and light. It's an all-time fave in our house. My mother will also appreciate this chapter as she has an unwritten rule that lunch should only be soup or a sandwich, or both if she is feeling exotic. Mum, there are many new soups for you to try in this chapter! Rock on!

Salads have always been a firm favourite with me, as I love the idea of chucking loads of different flavours and textures on a plate in the speediest of timeframes. A bit of crunch, a bit of a tang, a bit of sweetness. Anything goes! The Simple summer beetroot & orange salad on page 68 is so scrummy – I love the sweetness of the beets and the oranges. So fresh and vibrant, and it looks beautiful too. You may have heard people say that the brighter the food on your plate, the better it is for you; well, this dish couldn't be any more kaleidoscopic.

Every dish in this chapter is easy to make and is bursting with flavour and vitality. They all work well as side dishes, smart starters or light lunches that are quick, easy and heavenly on the tum.

SOUPS &
SALADS

VEGGIE VIETNAMESE SOUP

SERVES 4

My husband and I both adore this rich yet fresh soup. It's warming and reviving and is packed with protein due to the silken tofu. The spices give so much flavour to the body of this dish and marry perfectly with the broccoli and rice noodles. The traditional Vietnamese soup would be made with beef stock, but this is a vegetarian version for all my non-meat-eating friends out there.

2 litres fresh vegetable stock

1 onion, thinly sliced

3cm piece of root ginger, peeled and sliced

3 cloves garlic

2 tsp black peppercorns

2 sticks cinnamon

5 star anise

5 cloves

1½ tbsp coriander seeds

4 tbsp soy sauce

2 tbsp maple syrup or honey

375g flat rice noodles

80g tenderstem broccoli

200g silken tofu, drained and cut into cubes

100g bean sprouts

3 spring onions, sliced on the diagonal

Fresh herbs, mint, Thai basil, coriander, to serve

2 red chillies, sliced

2 limes, cut into wedges

Put the stock, onion, ginger, garlic and all the spices into a pan and bring to the boil. Reduce the heat and simmer for 30–40 minutes. Strain the broth through a fine sieve and return the liquid to the pot. Add the soy sauce and maple syrup or honey. Taste and adjust the seasoning with more of either if necessary. Bear in mind that if you are using instant stock that contains salt, you may not need any soy sauce at all, so be sure to taste prior to seasoning.

Cook the rice noodles according to the packet instructions, then plunge into cold water and separate to stop them from sticking. When ready to serve, bring the broth to a fast rolling boil, add the broccoli and tofu and cook for 1 minute. Distribute the noodles into four bowls, ladle over the boiling stock, broccoli and tofu and top with the bean sprouts, spring onions, herbs and chillies.

Serve immediately with the lime wedges.

BEETROOT, CHICKPEA & QUINOA SOUP

SERVES 6-8

I could eat beetroots until they come out of my ears. I love their colour, sweetness and all-round goodness. The beets give this soup a wonderfully comforting taste and accompany the other veg and flavours perfectly. This soup is quick and easy to make and has loads of vibrant veg, health-boosting chickpeas and protein-packed quinoa. It's filling and energy-boosting, so you can happily devour this knowing it'll see you through until your next meal.

2 tbsp olive oil

1 leek, trimmed and finely chopped

4 cloves garlic, crushed

3 cooked beetroots, roughly chopped

6 carrots, peeled and roughly chopped

2 litres vegetable stock

400g tin chickpeas, drained and rinsed

200g quinoa, rinsed

2 tbsp chives, finely chopped

Extra virgin olive oil, for drizzling

Sea salt and freshly ground black pepper

Put the oil in a large high-sided pot and set over a medium heat. Add the leek and sauté gently for 10 minutes until soft and golden. Add the crushed garlic and fry for another minute until aromatic.

Add the beetroots, carrots and vegetable stock and bring to a boil, then reduce the heat and simmer for 10 minutes. Add the chickpeas and quinoa and cook for a further 10–15 minutes until the quinoa and vegetables are cooked through.

Season to taste with up to 1½ teaspoons of salt and a good grinding of pepper (if you used instant stock it may not need any extra salt at all, so make sure to taste before seasoning).

Serve in bowls with the chives scattered over and a little drizzle of extra virgin olive oil.

The quinoa will continue to absorb the liquid in the soup after cooking, becoming thicker over time. If you prefer it thinner, simply add a little more stock.

THAI COCONUT SOUP

SERVES 4

This creamy, exotic-tasting soup awakens the taste buds as it is packed with flavour. The coconut milk gives you a dose of healthy fats and the lime and ginger are both wonderful tonics for when you're feeling run down. This is a great soup to make ahead of time as the flavours just keep on building, but it will of course taste divine eaten straight away too. If you eat meat you can use chicken stock instead of vegetable stock and add strips of chicken to chunk up the soup

1 litre vegetable stock

4cm piece of root ginger, peeled and sliced

3 cloves garlic, sliced

5 kaffir lime leaves

3 tbsp fish sauce

2 sticks of lemongrass, bruised

Juice of 2 limes

400ml tin coconut milk

3 red chillies, deseeded and finely sliced

Handful of fresh coriander or mint leaves, to serve (optional)

Put the vegetable stock, ginger, garlic, lime leaves, fish sauce, lemongrass, lime juice and coconut milk in a pot and bring to the boil.

Reduce the heat, add most of the chilli and simmer for 15 minutes. If you are serving the soup immediately, the ginger, lime leaves and lemongrass can be removed. If not, leave them in until you are ready to serve as they will continue to infuse the soup with flavour.

Serve in bowls with the remaining chilli and the coriander or mint on top, if you like.

FLEXI OPTION

Substitute the vegetable stock for chicken stock for a meatier flavour. You can also add in 250g of chicken breast cut into thin strips for some protein. Sauté the chicken slices in a little coconut oil for 2-3 minutes over a high heat until opaque. Add them to the soup after you've brought the liquid to the boil and before you add the chilli.

LENTIL WINTER WARMER SOUP

SERVES 4

This is one of the dishes made most often in our household. My little girl Honey loves dipping slices of toast into the soup's creaminess, and my husband and I both love to have this as a warming lunch on a cold day. It's very quick and easy to make and has a sweet flavour, due to the leek, onions and garlic. I adore this soup and love knowing I'm getting so many wonderful nutrients into my body in one hit.

1 tbsp olive oil or coconut oil

1 leek, trimmed and finely chopped

1 red onion, finely chopped

3 cloves garlic, crushed

1 litre vegetable stock

1 sweet potato, peeled and diced

1 carrot, peeled and diced

100g red lentils

Hummus (page 49 or shop-bought), to serve

1 tbsp extra virgin olive oil, plus extra for drizzling

½ tsp smoked paprika

1 tbsp roughly chopped chives

Bread, to serve (optional)

Sea salt and freshly ground black pepper

Put the oil in a large pot set over a medium heat. Add the leek and red onion and sauté for 5 minutes. Add the garlic and sweat out for another 5 minutes, until the onion and leek are translucent. Season well with salt and pepper.

Add the stock, sweet potato, carrot and lentils and bring to a boil. Skim off any foam that rises to the surface. Reduce the heat and simmer for 20–25 minutes until the vegetables and lentils are cooked through. Taste and adjust the seasoning if necessary with more salt and pepper. You may need up to half a teaspoon of salt if you used fresh, unsalted stock, or none at all if you used instant stock.

Transfer the soup to a blender and blitz until completely smooth (or blend in the pan with a stick blender).

Combine 2 tablespoons of hummus with the extra virgin olive oil, smoked paprika and 1 tablespoon of water. Divide the soup between four bowls, drizzle with the hummus and a few more drops of extra-virgin olive oil and scatter with chives.

Serve immediately, with bread if you like.

GET WELL SOON SOUP

SERVES 4

I made this for my husband when he was feeling run down last year, as he had little appetite but needed some goodness in his body. To save myself the bother of cooking the two of us separate meals I detoured from the well-trodden path of healing chicken soup (since I don't eat meat) and invented this little number. It's packed with freshness and nutrients and is so comforting to eat. It's essentially a chicken noodle soup minus the chicken. The flavours offer a warm hug and help to heal and soothe you when you're feeling a little under the weather. Perfect for a winter's night too.

2 tbsp coconut oil

1 red onion, finely sliced

2 cloves garlic, crushed

1 sweet potato, peeled and chopped

400g tin chickpeas, drained and rinsed

1 litre vegetable stock

150g tenderstem broccoli

195g tin sweetcorn, drained and rinsed

100g soba noodles

Large handful of kale, rinsed and dried, and tough stems removed, and chopped

Sea salt and freshly ground black pepper

Put the coconut oil in a pan and set over a medium heat. Add the onion and sauté for 10 minutes, until soft and translucent. Add the garlic and fry for another 2 minutes, until aromatic.

Add the sweet potato, chickpeas and stock. Bring to a boil, then reduce the heat to medium and simmer for 12 minutes.

Add the broccoli, sweetcorn and noodles and simmer for 5 minutes, then add the kale and cook for a further 2–4 minutes, or until the sweet potato and noodles are cooked through (the time will vary depending on the brand of soba noodles you are using).

Season to taste with salt and pepper, bearing in mind that you may not need much salt if you used instant stock.

Serve immediately in bowls.

GINGER & LIME TOFU NOODLE SALAD

SERVES 4

This zingy salad always gives me a huge sensory wake-up. Its flavours are so fresh and punchy that it's impossible to be distracted when eating this dish. I find it handy to prep all the veg before you start cooking the tofu, as you want to chuck it all in at the same time towards the end of cooking.

400g firm tofu

2 tbsp vegetable oil

2 cloves garlic, crushed

1 stick of lemongrass, outer layers removed and tender core very finely chopped

3 shallots or 1 small red onion, finely sliced

2cm piece of root ginger, peeled and finely grated

1 red chilli, deseeded and finely sliced

4 lime leaves, very finely sliced (optional)

180g rice vermicelli noodles

60g rocket

150g firm mango, diced

80g roasted cashews or peanuts

15g fresh mint leaves

For the dressing:

1½ tbsp coconut palm sugar, maple syrup or honey

2 tbsp fish sauce

Grated zest of 1 lime

3 tbsp lime juice

1 tsp toasted sesame oil

Tightly wrap a clean tea towel around the tofu. Over a sink, squeeze the tofu very firmly, tightening the tea towel as you go, to extract as much water as possible, almost wringing out the tofu. Unwrap the tofu and crumble it into a bowl, breaking up any larger pieces with a fork.

Heat the oil in a large pan over a high heat. Add the crumbled tofu and stir-fry for 4 minutes until beginning to crisp up. Add the garlic, lemongrass, shallots or onion, grated ginger, most of the chilli and the lime leaves (if using), and stir-fry for another 1–2 minutes until fragrant. Keep everything moving the whole time to avoid burning. Transfer to a bowl and set aside.

Put the noodles in a large bowl and cover with boiling water. Test the noodles after 2–3 minutes to make sure they are cooked through, then drain well.

Add the noodles to the cooked tofu and toss with the rocket, mango, nuts, most of the mint and all of the dressing ingredients. Transfer to a serving dish and top with the remaining mint and chilli.

FLEXI OPTION

If you're cooking for meat-lovers, you can swap the tofu for minced pork and cook in the same way.

FIG & GREEN BEAN SALAD

SERVES 4

I knocked up this recipe when I had a gathering at our house last summer. When I am faced with big groups of hungry faces I prefer to make up big serving plates so everyone can dig in and help themselves. I made a huge version of this salad and it vanished in minutes. It's a juicy and flavoursome salad that is wonderful on a hot summer's day. The greens give this dish some bite and the figs and cheese deliver a melt-in-the-mouth quality. This is one of my all-time faves!

200g green beans, topped and tailed

200g rocket or lamb's lettuce, or both

6 figs, quartered

100g feta

4 tbsp salsa verde (page 74)

Sea salt and freshly ground black pepper

Put the green beans in a sieve positioned inside a saucepan filled with a little water, making sure that the water does not touch the bottom of the sieve. Place a lid over the beans and set the pan over a high heat. Steam the beans for 6 minutes, until tender. Alternatively, you can blanch the beans. Remove from the heat and set to one side.

To serve, layer the leaves, beans, figs and feta on to a large serving platter. Drizzle the salsa verde over the salad and toss together. Serve immediately.

CARROT, AVOCADO & TOFU SALAD

SERVES 4

Tofu sometimes gets a bad rep as it can be tasteless and bland when not cooked well. In this dish the tofu is the main event, and rightly so. It's bursting with flavour and texture, as the juicy marinade brings the tofu to life and the crisp coconut crust gives it a divine crunch. It's fresh and light – and quick to make if you can marinate the tofu the night before.

400g firm tofu
Extra virgin olive oil
1 tbsp balsamic vinegar
4 carrots, peeled
4 tbsp coconut flour
4 tbsp olive oil
2 avocado, peeled, halved, stone removed and sliced
Sesame seeds, to serve
Sea salt and freshly ground black pepper

For the dressing:
1 tbsp almond butter
2 tbsp extra virgin olive oil
2 tsp toasted sesame oil

To make the dressing, combine all the ingredients and set to one side.

Gently wrap the tofu in a clean tea towel. Place it on a chopping board and balance another chopping board or heavy plate on top. Leave to one side for 10 minutes to drain.

Meanwhile, in a bowl combine 2 tablespoons of olive oil, the balsamic vinegar and a pinch of salt and pepper. Cut the drained tofu into 1cm cubes and add to the bowl. Gently combine with the marinade, cover and leave for at least 1 hour to marinate, or overnight.

Half an hour before you plan on serving the dish, spiralise the carrots and toss with 1 tablespoon of olive oil, making sure they are well coated. Season to taste.

Remove the tofu cubes from the marinade and place in a clean bowl with the coconut flour. Toss them together to coat the tofu. Add the olive oil to a pan and set over a medium heat. Remove the tofu from the flour, discarding anything remaining, and fry in the pan for 10 minutes, turning now and again, until crispy and golden.

Divide the spiralised carrots between plates and top with the sliced avocado and the crispy tofu. Sprinkle over the sesame seeds, drizzle over the dressing and serve immediately.

SIMPLE SUMMER BEETROOT & ORANGE SALAD

SERVES 2

Having a very sweet tooth means I often subliminally make many of my savoury dishes lean strongly in this direction. This salad is so juicy and sweet as the oranges burst with flavour and colour, and the honey dressing delivers more wonderful sweetness. This is gorgeous as a quick lunch or a fresh side salad on a hot day.

150g quinoa, rinsed

Grated zest of 1 orange, with flesh separated into segments

2 tbsp extra virgin olive oil

1 tsp lemon juice

1 tsp honey

140g baby spinach leaves, rinsed and drained

1 raw beetroot, peeled and grated

Handful of toasted flaked almonds

Sea salt and freshly ground black pepper

In a saucepan (with a lid) bring the quinoa to a boil in double its quantity of salted water. Once it has come to the boil, reduce the heat to low, keep the lid on and cook for about 12 minutes until all the water has been absorbed. Remove from the heat and leave to one side.

In a bowl combine the orange zest, olive oil, lemon juice and honey and season with salt and pepper. Add this to the quinoa and stir to combine. Taste and adjust the seasoning if necessary.

Layer the quinoa, spinach, orange segments and grated beetroot on a serving dish. Sprinkle over the flaked almonds and serve immediately.

RUNNER BEAN SALAD

SERVES 2

Sometimes the simplest of dishes remain an all-time fave. I love this salad as an easy lunch in a hurry or as a side dish to a delicious main. If like me you adore goat's cheese, then crumble away to your heart's content. The creaminess of the cheese melts over these crunchy, flavour-packed greens beautifully.

1 tbsp olive oil

1 leek, halved lengthways, washed and thinly sliced

1 courgette, diced

250g runner beans, topped and tailed

3 cloves garlic, crushed

80g goat's cheese, crumbled

1 tbsp flaked almonds, toasted

Sea salt and freshly ground black pepper

Put the oil in a pan and set over a medium heat. Add the leek and courgette and sauté for 5 minutes until softened.

While the leek and courgette are cooking, cut the runner beans on an angle into 5cm pieces.

Add the beans to the pan and continue to sauté gently for a further 10 minutes, then add the garlic and sauté for another 2 minutes. The runner beans should still retain some crunch. Season to taste with salt and pepper.

Serve warm topped with the flaked almonds and goat's cheese.

BUTTERNUT SQUASH & KALE WARMING SALAD

SERVES 4

This salad is particularly pretty and is very easy to make. Because the squash is sliced thinly there is no need to remove the skin, it just gives the dish more texture. The pomegranate adds even more vibrancy to this dish as the little red gems add a burst of juice to proceedings. It's a filling, healthy, quick and easy lunch or light dinner.

300g quinoa, rinsed

1 small butternut squash, deseeded and cut into 1cm slices (no need to peel)

2½ tbsp olive oil

80g kale, rinsed and dried, tough stems removed, and roughly chopped

2 corn cobs, or 150g sweetcorn, drained and rinsed

Handful of fresh flat-leaf parsley leaves, roughly chopped

5 tbsp Smoked paprika & tahini dressing (page 75)

Sea salt and freshly ground black pepper

Preheat the oven to 200°C/180°C fan/ 400°F/Gas mark 6.

In a saucepan (with a lid), bring the quinoa to the boil in double its quantity of salted water. Once it has come to the boil, reduce the heat to low, keep the lid on and cook for about 12 minutes until all the water has been absorbed. Remove from the heat and leave to one side.

Place the squash on a baking tray, coat with 2 tablespoons of the olive oil and season generously with salt and pepper. Roast for 15 minutes, then stir in the kale and roast for a further 5 minutes until the squash is golden and cooked through.

While the squash is roasting, bring a large pan of salted water to the boil and cook the corn cobs for 6 minutes. Drain well, then place a griddle pan over a high heat. Rub the remaining half tablespoon of oil over the corn and season with salt and pepper. Once the griddle pan is hot, add the corn and cook on each side for about 2 minutes, until slightly charred. With a knife carefully remove the corn kernels from the cob and set to one side. Alternatively, use tinned sweetcorn.

Stir most of the parsley into the quinoa, then layer it on a large serving platter with the squash, kale and corn. Drizzle the smoked paprika & tahini dressing over the salad. Finish by scattering over the remaining parsley.

SALSA VERDE

A friend of mine, Antonia Parker, who is a brilliant chef, recently made me and my family the most incredible meal for my husbands fortieth birthday. The star of the show was her salsa verde. I dolloped it over everything with glee. After this meal I went about trying to perfect my own delicious salsa verde, and I'm very happy with this concoction. It's a perfect accompaniment to salads – as well as vegetable dishes and white fish. It is irresistible!

2 anchovy fillets, finely chopped

25g fresh flat-leaf parsley leaves, chopped

25g fresh basil leaves, chopped

Grated zest of 1 lemon

1 clove garlic

2 tbsp red wine vinegar

140ml extra virgin olive oil

2 tbsp capers, drained

Sea salt, to taste

Put the anchovy fillets, herbs, lemon zest and garlic in the bowl of a food processor and pulse on and off until you have a rough paste.

Drizzle in the red wine vinegar, olive oil and the capers, pulsing on and off, until you have a rough herb oil. You can add a little more oil to thin it out if you prefer.

Taste and adjust the seasoning if necessary with a little more vinegar or with salt.

SMOKED PAPRIKA & TAHINI DRESSING

MAKES ABOUT 100ML

This punchy dressing works so well with salads and quinoa dishes. I adore tahini for its creaminess as well as for its health-boosting properties. The paprika adds a kick and gives this dressing an extra boost of flavour. I often find shop-bought dressings are packed with salt and make me feel very bloated, so I always prefer to make my own as they taste better and I know exactly what has gone into them.

60ml tahini
1 clove garlic, crushed
1 tbsp lemon juice
1 tbsp extra virgin olive oil
½ tsp smoked paprika
Pinch of sea salt and freshly ground black pepper

Mix together all of the ingredients in a bowl until thoroughly combined. Keep whisking in a tablespoon of water until you reach your desired consistency.

Store in an airtight container in the fridge for up to a week.

Is it just me or do lunches seem to be getting shorter? Whenever I go abroad I adore how lunch still seems to be savoured, cherished and enjoyed at a slow-motion pace. Glorious.

Back home we all seem to have far less time for it, not just in terms of what we eat and when, but even how we eat it. Are you one of those people who grabs a sandwich from a nearby shop and eats it as you walk? Do you skip your lunch break at work to get more done, so end up throwing food down your throat without giving your brain a chance to switch off? Do you have small kids who need feeding themselves, so your needs get somewhat pushed aside? Maybe it's not that easy to chill out over lunch after all! It's definitely worth a try though, and these quick and easy recipes should give you a helping hand.

I make lunch from scratch most days, as I prefer to know what's going into my meals, and also because I usually eat lunch with my kids so I love them to watch me do it. I hope this will entice them into cooking themselves down the line. I love watching them eat my home-cooked food, as it makes me happy seeing they're getting fresh ingredients in their systems.

On days when I'm out of the house for work I'll always try to make lunch for myself while I'm making the kids their breakfast. I'll whip up something quickly, like the Tuna & cannellini bean lunchbox salad on page 95, and pop it in my bag for later. SO much more cost-effective than buying something whilst I'm out, and healthier too. If I'm at home on my own I'll make myself a meal that is bursting with flavour and energy – possibly something I can make or adapt for the kids at another time.

At this point in the day you're still only halfway through what needs doing, so your energy levels need to be lifted and sustained. The lunches in this chapter feature a variety of freshness, protein and vibrancy to give you that half-time boost. The afternoon is when most of us tend to slump somewhat and lose momentum in our motivation. A good lunch packed with nutritious ingredients can be the helping hand in keeping our focus and good moods on track.

LUNCH
ON THE RUN

LEEK &
COURGETTE
PASTA

SERVES 6

One way to get a host of vegetables into your daily routine is to make a glorious pasta dish. This recipe is loaded with an assortment of brightly coloured veg to benefit your body and mind in many ways. You can cook this up the night before and pop it in a Tupperware container for the following day, which speeds things up dramatically. If, like my own kids, yours take a little encouragement to eat veg, then blend up the sauce before adding the pasta for a wonderful hidden-veg sauce.

2 tbsp olive oil

2 leeks, trimmed, halved lengthways and finely sliced

2 courgettes, diced

2 carrots, peeled and diced

3 cloves garlic, crushed

150g broccoli florets

400g tin chopped tomatoes

350g spelt, rice or quinoa fusilli pasta

1 tbsp extra virgin olive oil

1 ball of buffalo mozzarella, torn into chunks

Handful of fresh basil leaves, to serve

Sea salt and freshly ground black pepper

Place a large pot of water on to boil.

Put the olive oil in a pan and set over a medium heat. Add the leeks, courgettes and carrots and sauté for 10 minutes. Add the garlic and broccoli and fry for another 2 minutes. Pour over the chopped tomatoes and simmer gently for 10 minutes until the vegetables are cooked through. Season to taste with salt and pepper.

Meanwhile, once the water has come to the boil, add 2 teaspoons of salt and the pasta. Cook until al dente, according to the packet instructions.

Once cooked, drain the pasta and add it to the sauce together with the extra virgin olive oil. Toss to coat, then serve immediately with the mozzarella and basil scattered over, or leave to cool and store in a Tupperware container as a packed lunch.

CAULIFLOWER-RICE-STUFFED TOMATOES

SERVES 4

If time is tight in your busy morning schedule this is the perfect lunch to make the night before, as the flavours just keep building. Once you've prepared the tomatoes, leave them in the fridge overnight and then serve them up at lunchtime, or pop them in a container to take to work. I love cauliflower rice as it gets even more veg in your diet and it adds extra flavour to this recipe. I tend to make a huge batch of cauliflower rice and then freeze it to use whenever I need it. I love the combination of tomato, basil and mozarella – and would recommend not holding back when piling the latter on!

500g cauliflower florets

1 tsbp olive oil

1 leek, trimmed and finely chopped

8 large beef tomatoes

2 cloves garlic, crushed

1 tsp fresh rosemary leaves, finely chopped

Small handful of fresh basil leaves, finely chopped

60g grated mozarella (optional)

Sea salt and freshly ground black pepper

Preheat the oven to 200°C/180°C fan/400°F/Gas mark 6.

Put the cauliflower florets in the bowl of a food processor and pulse until you have grains the size of rice. Set to one side.

Add the oil to a pan and set over a medium heat. Add the leek and sauté for 5 minutes until beginning to soften.

Meanwhile, slice off the tops of the tomatoes. With a teaspoon, carefully scoop out the juicy inner flesh and seeds of the tomatoes and transfer to the pan, together with the garlic, rosemary and basil. Season and continue to sauté with the leeks for another 5 minutes until the leeks are cooked and the tomato has reduced down. Add the cauliflower rice and stir to combine. Cook for another 2 minutes until the cauliflower is beginning to soften. Season again to taste with salt and pepper.

Season the inside of the hulled tomatoes, and stuff with the cauliflower rice. Keep aside any leftover cauliflower rice. Transfer the tomatoes to a baking tray and scatter over the grated mozarella, if using. Bake for 15 minutes until the tomatoes are cooked through and just holding their shape. Serve immediately with a green salad, or leave to cool completely and eat at room temperature the next day.

HOT SMOKED SALMON OPEN-FACED SANDWICH

MAKES 1 LARGE SANDWICH

To me the word 'sandwich' is synonymous with a floppy cheese-and-cucumber slice found at the bottom of my school bag. This sandwich is the absolute opposite of that and oozes sophistication and beauty. The crème fraiche is loaded with flavour and each bite of this dish offers up something different, from the sun-dried tomatoes to the crunch of the cucumber. Toast the bread for extra crunch and pack up this dreamboat in a container for the day ahead.

½ tsp cumin seeds

2 tbsp crème fraiche or yoghurt (Greek or soy)

1 small clove garlic, crushed

1 tsp good-quality balsamic vinegar

10 chives, roughly chopped

2 slices of sourdough, spelt or gluten-free bread

20g lamb's lettuce or rocket

100g hot smoked salmon fillets, broken into flakes

¼ cucumber, halved lengthways and sliced

6 semi-dried tomatoes

Sea salt and freshly ground black pepper

Put the cumin seeds in a dry pan over a medium heat and fry for 2 minutes or until aromatic. Remove to a pestle and mortar and roughly bash the seeds to release the flavour. Combine the cumin with the crème fraiche or yoghurt, garlic, balsamic vinegar and most of the chives.

Slather the crème fraiche or yoghurt over the 2 slices of bread, top with the lettuce or rocket, salmon, cucumber, semi-dried tomatoes and the remaining chives. Season with a little salt and pepper and serve immediately.

If you are making this for a packed lunch, keep the crème fraiche or yoghurt in a jar and the bread and topping ingredients in a lunch box. Assemble just before you plan on eating.

STUFFED AVOCADOS

SERVES 2

The avocado is still having a moment, so here's another idea for how to enjoy this delicious favourite. The hot veg works really well with the creaminess of the avocado flesh, but if you are planning to take this out for the day with you, prepare the veg and store it in a container and leave the avocado whole until you sit down to enjoy your lunch. That way it won't go brown and will taste as fresh as can be.

1 tbsp olive oil

1 leek, trimmed and finely sliced

1 courgette, diced

100g cherry tomatoes, halved

2 cloves garlic, crushed

2 ripe avocados

60g feta, crumbled

¼ tsp smoked paprika

1 tbsp fresh flat-leaf parsley leaves, finely chopped

Extra virgin olive oil, for drizzling

Sea salt and freshly ground black pepper

Put the oil in a pan set over a medium heat. Add the leek and sweat down for 5 minutes. Add the courgette and sauté for another 5 minutes, then add the tomatoes and garlic and cook for 2 more minutes until aromatic. Season to taste with salt and pepper.

When ready to serve, halve the avocados and remove the stone. Divide the vegetable mixture between the halves and top with the feta, smoked paprika, parsley and a drizzle of extra virgin olive oil.

FRIED ASPARAGUS & COURGETTE CHIP SALAD

SERVES 2

This is great as a quick lunch or a lovely side dish, or as a big serving platter for a group of guests. I started breadcrumb-coating every vegetable in sight once I had kids, in an attempt to get them eating more veg. The Parmesan gives these veggie sticks loads of dreamy flavour and crunch, with the added bonus of getting a whole lot of green goodness into your diet.

1 courgette, topped and tailed

60g breadcrumbs (gluten-free if you prefer)

35g grated Parmesan cheese, or nutritional yeast, plus extra to serve

100g asparagus spears

50g white spelt flour or gluten-free flour

1 egg, beaten

2 tbsp olive oil

80g cherry tomatoes, halved

100g rocket

Extra virgin olive oil, for drizzling

Balsamic vinegar, for drizzling

Sea salt and freshly ground black pepper

Halve the courgette lengthways and slice into 1cm-thick strips.

Combine the breadcrumbs and Parmesan cheese or nutritional yeast in a bowl. Dip the asparagus and courgette strips into the flour, followed by the beaten egg and then coat with the breadcrumbs.

Heat the olive oil in a pan. Add the courgette and asparagus in batches, and fry for 2–3 minutes on each side until cooked through and golden. Remove to a piece of kitchen paper.

Combine the tomatoes, rocket, courgette and asparagus. Sprinkle over a little more Parmesan cheese or nutritional yeast and drizzle with extra virgin olive oil and balsamic vinegar. Serve immediately.

PRAWN, AVOCADO & LEMON MAYO WRAP

SERVES 1

Surely the wrap is the easiest and quickest lunch on the run. Fill it, roll it, run with it. This homemade wrap will be a lot less soggy but a lot more packed than your shop-bought version, and is light and nutritious yet filling too. I'm a bit of a wimp when it comes to chilli, but boost the spice level of yours as desired. The lemony yoghurt is a real treat too!

3 tbsp Greek yoghurt

Grated zest of ½ unwaxed lemon

1 clove garlic, crushed

1 ripe avocado, halved and stoned

1 large wholegrain or gluten-free wrap

Small handful of mixed leaves

80g cooked and peeled king prawns

Dried chilli flakes (optional)

Sea salt and freshly ground black pepper

Combine the yoghurt, lemon zest and garlic in a bowl and season to taste with salt and pepper.

Peel the skin off the avocado, slice and set to one side. Warm the wrap in a dry pan set over a medium heat.

Spread the yoghurt over the wrap and top with the mixed leaves, avocado, prawns and some dried chilli flakes (if using). Season with salt and pepper, then fold over the wrap to enclose the filling and serve immediately.

ASIAN MARINATED TOFU

WITH GREENS AND BROWN RICE

SERVES 2

This is the perfect, quick yet nutritious lunch for when time is tight – it can be popped in a Tupperware container to take with you if you're going to be out and about, or assembled and eaten at home with minimal fuss. I usually have some marinated tofu in my fridge as I use it in so many recipes, which makes this lunch even quicker to prepare. Marinate the tofu overnight, then you can pop it on a plate quickly when hunger strikes. If you have some leftover quinoa or brown rice then they make a perfect accompaniment to the flavoursome tofu.

350g silken tofu

1½ tbsp rice vinegar

2 tbsp tamari or soy sauce

2 tbsp extra virgin olive oil

1 tsp maple syrup or honey

1 clove garlic, crushed

1 spring onion, finely chopped

70g baby spinach leaves, rinsed and drained

Toasted sesame seeds, for sprinkling

Cooked brown rice or quinoa, to serve

Slice the tofu into 1cm-thick slices and lay them flat in a wide dish or Tupperware container.

Whisk together the rice vinegar, tamari or soy sauce, olive oil, maple syrup or honey, garlic and most of the spring onions in a bowl. Pour over the tofu, cover and leave to marinate in the fridge for 4–6 hours, or ideally overnight.

To serve, divide the spinach leaves between two plates, top with the tofu and sauce and sprinkle over the remaining spring onions and a pinch of sesame seeds. Serve with the cooked brown rice or quinoa on the side.

FLEXI OPTION

Swap the tofu for 4 boneless chicken thighs cut into bitesize chunks, then marinate as per the recipe. When ready, roast at 180℃ fan oven for 20-25 minutes until cooked through. Serve as per the tofu, and drizzle over a little more olive oil if needed, as the marinade will reduce during cooking.

RAINBOW STIR-FRY

SERVES 4

What's not to love about a stir-fry? When you really can't be bothered to cook for ages and have a hunger on, the stir-fry comes to the rescue. Get all your veg prepped and chopped first so you can swiftly chuck them all in the pan, then let the flavours work their magic on this crunchy, nutritious dish.

1 tbsp coconut oil or sunflower oil

3cm piece of root ginger, peeled and sliced into think matchsticks

3 cloves garlic, thinly sliced

1 red pepper, deseeded and thinly sliced

100g mange tout, thinly sliced

1 red chilli, deseeded and thinly sliced

150g prawns

1½ tbsp tamarind

2 tsp toasted sesame oil

1 tsp toasted sesame seeds, to serve

Cooked brown rice, to serve

Put the coconut oil or olive oil in a large pan or wok and set over a high heat. Once very hot, add the ginger, garlic, pepper, mange tout and chilli. Stir-fry, keeping everything on the move all the time, for 2 minutes. Add the prawns and stir-fry for another minute. Add the tamarind and cook for a further 2 minutes until the prawns are cooked through.

Remove from the heat and stir in the sesame oil. Plate up the rice and spoon over the stir-fry. Sprinkle with sesame seeds and serve immediately.

TUNA & CANNELLINI BEAN LUNCHBOX SALAD

SERVES 2

This is a superhero lunchbox packed with protein from the tuna and healthy slow-release carbs from the beans. It's fresh and flavoursome and reminds me of a Mediterranean lunch on holiday. It's perfect to pack in a Tupperware container for the day ahead, but is equally as wonderful to enjoy at home.
It's a great sharing dish too, if you double up the quantities and serve it in a large bowl for anyone coming over for dinner. If you prefer you can use fresh tuna steak instead of tinned tuna: simply cook on a high heat in a glug of oil for a few minutes on each side, then flake over the other ingredients.

200g tuna in olive oil, drained and broken into chunks

½ red onion, thinly sliced

80g cherry tomatoes, halved

½ red pepper, deseeded and thinly sliced

400g tin cannellini beans, drained and rinsed

Small handful of fresh flat-leaf parsley leaves, chopped

Grated zest of 1 unwaxed lemon and 1 tbsp juice

2 tbsp extra virgin olive oil

1 clove garlic, crushed

1 tsp honey

1 tsp wholegrain mustard

80g rocket

Sea salt and freshly ground black pepper

Combine the tuna, red onion, tomatoes, red pepper, cannellini beans and parsley in a bowl.

In a separate bowl, combine the lemon zest, juice, olive oil, garlic, honey, wholegrain mustard and season with salt and pepper to taste.

If you plan on taking this as a packed lunch, store the dressing in a jar and keep the tuna salad and rocket leaves separate in a lunchbox. When you are ready to eat, combine the rocket and tuna salad with the dressing.

If you are eating at home, put the rocket on a serving platter, top with the tuna and bean salad and drizzle over the dressing.

SMOKED TOFU, AUBERGINE & SPINACH

WITH SOBA NOODLES

SERVES 4

I instantly smile when I think of a giant bowl of this goodness. This is a quick and easy hot lunch that will warm your bones and fill you with good, slow-release energy. The aubergines give this dish so much flavour and depth and complement the spinach and balsamic vinegar perfectly. I'm getting hungry just thinking about it!

300g soba noodles

6 tbsp olive oil

2 aubergine, sliced into thin rounds

150g smoked tofu

1 tbsp balsamic vinegar

15g fresh flat-leaf parsley leaves, finely chopped

200g spinach leaves

250g roasted red peppers from a jar, sliced

Parmesan cheese, to serve (optional)

Sea salt and freshly ground black pepper

Cook the noodles according to the packet instructions, rinse in cold water, drain and toss with a little olive oil to prevent sticking. Leave to one side.

Brush the aubergine slices on both sides with 3 tablespoons of the oil. Add them to a large frying pan and set over a medium-high heat. Cook for 3–4 minutes on each side, until soft and golden. Season well and set aside.

Add the smoked tofu to the same pan and set over a high heat. Cook for 3–4 minutes, tossing every now and again, until crispy. Set aside, and keep any of the fat that has rendered off.

Combine the vinegar, most of the parsley and the remaining olive oil in a bowl and season to taste.

Add the spinach to a large pan set over a high heat. Cook for 2–3 minutes, tossing now and again, until the spinach has wilted down. Add the soba noodles to the pan together with the olive oil dressing, aubergines, red peppers and smoked tofu. Toss everything together over a medium heat until warmed through.

Season to taste and add in a little Parmesan, if you like. Serve in a large serving bowl with the remaining parsley scattered over.

The 4 p.m. slump is a bore. You can sense it coming, knowing that you're in for an internal battle over whether or not to eat your way through a packet of biscuits. Your energy is low: you've conquered 75 per cent of your day but you still need a little help to get over the finish line. The afternoon treat is the perfect solution to this sloth-like portion of the day – and the recipes I've included here also cut out the inner battle, as all of these treats are packed with goodness! Snacks don't need to ruin your evening meal or give you a sugar high too late in the day. You can make these treats in your spare time and take them to work with you, or simply store them at home for when the moment strikes.

I gave up refined sugar after my first child, Rex, was born. I had been feeling particularly sluggish after six months of breastfeeding and eating my way down the biscuit aisle. I needed a pep-up and I needed it to be easy as I had my hands full with my new little partner in crime. Cutting out refined sugar seemed like one easy rule I could stick to. The first two weeks were the toughest, while my body acclimatised. At this point I hadn't discovered how easily you could make treats that were sweet but still relatively virtuous. Creating sweet treats with natural sugars has become one of my favourite hobbies as I can feed my sweet tooth, offer up less sugar-laden treats to my kids and watch my mates'

faces stretch out in shock when I tell them how saintly my snacks are. The Choccie biccies on page 102 are one of my son's absolute faves. He loves making these with me – but really he prefers just scoffing them! Knowing that they're not full of refined white sugar makes life much easier, as he is less likely to have an uncontrollable sugar-hyper half-hour, yet they still taste naughty. Win-win!

The Chocolate milk on page 113 is savoured by all in the Wood household. The kids love it and drink it most afternoons, I love it and could drink it by the gallon and my husband gulps it down after a cycle round the park. It's creamy and dreamy and has hidden spinach that you can't see or taste. It's sneakily hiding behind a whole army of flavours, yet remains powerful in its source of vitamins.

Afternoon treats go hand-in-hand with our Great British pastime of tea-drinking, so you'll also find some soothing and refreshing hot drinks in this chapter too. Welcome to afternoon bliss!

AFTERNOON
TREATS

CASHEW, CHIA & CRANBERRY BRITTLE

SERVES 6

This brittle is the ultimate treat. From the initial snap to the chewy chomp, this luxurious sweet treat is best savoured with a cup of warm tea and a loved one close by to share it with. I also love to make this as a gift for a friend; wrapped in Cellophane and secured with a bow it makes a pretty and tasty, non-expensive present. But if you can't bear to part with it just store it in a container to nibble on whenever the mood takes you.

150g raw unsalted cashew nuts, roughly chopped

40g oats

3 tbsp chia seeds

75g dried cranberries

½ tsp ground cinnamon

30g coconut palm sugar

3 tbsp coconut oil or unsalted butter

100ml brown rice syrup or maple syrup

¾ tsp sea salt

Preheat the oven to 160°C/140°C fan/320°F/Gas mark 3 and line a baking tray with baking parchment.

Combine the cashews, oats, chia seeds, dried cranberries, cinnamon, coconut palm sugar and salt in a bowl.

Melt the coconut oil or butter in a pan over a low heat. Add the brown rice syrup or maple syrup and stir to combine.

Pour this into the cashew mixture and thoroughly combine, ensuring that all the nuts, seeds and oats are fully coated.

Using the back of a spoon, spread the mixture out on the lined baking tray, to a thickness of about half a centimetre. Bake in the oven for 25–30 minutes until golden. Remove from the oven and leave to cool completely.

When the brittle has cooled, break it into shards and store in an airtight container in the fridge for up to 2 weeks.

REX'S FAVOURITE CHOCCIE BICCIES

MAKES 20-24 BISCUITS
OF DIFFERENT
SHAPES AND SIZES

I must have made these biscuits at least fifty times, as it is essential that our biccie tin is always full of them. Although I've named them Rex's faves, they are actually devoured and loved by all in our house. They're very easy and enjoyable to make with little ones too. Rex loves to help me stir the mixture and cut the dough into different shapes. Kids' sweet treats don't have to be laden with refined sugars and E numbers: this simple yet divine recipe is an all-round family pleaser and won't leave you with a sugar-crazed high.

125g unsalted butter or coconut oil
125g coconut palm sugar
1 egg
½ tsp vanilla extract
200g rice flour
½ tsp baking powder
50g raw cacao powder or unsweetened cocoa powder
Pinch of sea salt

Preheat the oven to 200°C/180°C fan/400°F/Gas mark 6 and line a baking tray with baking parchment.

In a large bowl, cream together the butter or coconut oil and the sugar. Beat in the egg and vanilla extract, followed by the flour, baking powder, salt and cacao powder or cocoa powder, until the mixture comes together as a dough. Cover with cling film and refrigerate for 20 minutes.

Once chilled but still pliable, roll out the dough to a thickness of 1cm. With a cookie cutter of your choice, cut out as many biscuits as you can, then bring the remaining dough back together, roll out again and cut out the remaining biscuits.

Place on the baking tray and bake for 8–10 minutes until dry and biscuity in appearance. Remove from the oven and leave to cool for 10 minutes. Transfer to a cooling rack and leave to cool completely.

Store in an airtight container for up to 1 week.

RAW FLAPJACKS

MAKES 15 FLAPJACKS

These have got to be the quickest snacks to make ever. Just blend up all the ingredients and you're good to go! They're perfect to keep in the fridge to ward off an afternoon energy slump. The oats will give you a boost for the rest of the day and the goji berries will provide some much-needed vitamin C. If you have more time you can decorate with the toppings I've suggested, both of which gives these delicious flapjacks even more flavour.

160g oats
10 Medjool dates, pitted
4 tbsp coconut oil, melted
2 tbsp goji berries, plus extra for scattering
80g desiccated coconut
Pinch of sea salt

To decorate (optional):
20g dark chocolate, melted
or
1 tbsp coconut oil, melted
2 tsp unsweetened cocoa powder
1 tsp honey or maple syrup
Pinch of sea salt

Line a 24 x 16cm baking tray or Tupperware box with baking parchment.

Place all the flapjack ingredients in the bowl of a food processor and blitz for 1–2 minutes until they come together when pressed between your fingers.

Flatten the mixture into the lined baking tray or Tupperware box, scatter over a few more goji beries and press them into the flapjack. Cover and refrigerate for 30 minutes, or place in the freezer for 10 minutes.

Gently pull up the baking parchment to release the flattened mixture. Cut into 15 squares of equal size.

To decorate, drizzle over the melted chocolate. Alternatively combine the coconut oil, cocoa powder, honey or maple syrup and salt and drizzle over. Leave to set, then stack the flapjacks on top of one another and serve.

SWEET POTATO SCONES

MAKES 8 SCONES

I don't think I ate a sweet potato until I was well into my twenties. Growing up it was jacket spuds all the way, so I'm not sure I'd even heard of sweet potatoes until I went to the States. I wonder how I coped without them as I now eat them almost every day! My daughter loves them blended with a little butter, we all love them as fries and I adore baking with them. They add nutrients to your sweet treats and have the perfect consistency for these little scones. A scone and cup of tea around 4 p.m. is bliss.

2 large sweet potatoes

50ml maple syrup or honey

1 egg, beaten

250g white spelt flour, plus extra for rolling

30g coconut palm sugar

2 tsp baking powder

½ tsp ground cinnamon

60g coconut oil or unsalted butter

½ tsp sea salt

Salted butter or coconut oil, to serve

Jam or almond butter, to serve

Preheat the oven to 180°C/160°C fan/350°F/Gas mark 4 and line a baking tray with baking parchment.

Wrap the sweet potatoes in foil and roast in the oven for about an hour (depending on their size) until completely cooked through. Remove from the oven, discard the foil and cut the potatoes in half lengthways and leave to cool. Once completely cold, scoop out 250g of the soft flesh. Use any remaining sweet potato in a salad. Add the 250g of flesh to the bowl of a food processor with the maple syrup or honey and purée until smooth. Add the egg and process for a few seconds, just until combined.

Combine the flour, sugar, baking powder, salt and cinnamon in a bowl. Rub in the coconut oil or butter until it looks like breadcrumbs. Gradually stir in the sweet potato mixture a little at a time, until you have an evenly moist, smooth dough. It should not be wet or sticky and you may not need to add all the sweet potato mixture, as some potatoes will have a higher water content than others.

Turn the dough out on to a lightly floured work surface and roll or pat out (with floured hands) to a thickness of 2.5cm. Use a 6cm round pastry cutter (either clean-edged or fluted) to punch out as many scones as possible, dipping the cutter into flour as you go, before cutting, to prevent it sticking to the dough. Use up all the leftover scraps of dough, rolling it out again and punching out scones as before. Arrange on the baking tray and place in the centre of the oven. Bake for 12–15 minutes until risen and golden brown in colour.

Remove to a wire rack and leave to cool a little. Serve warm with butter or coconut oil and your favourite jam or almond butter. Store in an airtight container and consume within 2 days.

SAVOURY POPCORN

SERVES 2

Shop-bought popcorn is usually drenched in refined sugar or tons of salt, so is not always the best option for an afternoon pick-me-up. This popcorn recipe is abundant in flavour yet kind to the body: the perfect afternoon snack attack. Make a load of this and store it in an airtight jar for all-day snacking or for sharing with your friends and family.

1 tbsp vegetable oil
50g popping corn
1 tsp ground cumin
1 tsp smoked paprika
½ tsp garlic powder
1 tbsp maple syrup or honey
1 tbsp olive oil
½ tsp sea salt

Heat the vegetable oil in a large pan (with a lid) set over a medium heat. Add the corn kernels and place the lid on top immediately. Shake the pan a little so that the corn is coated in the oil.

Cook for 4–5 minutes, shaking the pan every now and again, until the popping has almost stopped. Remove from the heat and transfer the popcorn to a large mixing bowl.

In another bowl combine the ground cumin, smoked paprika, garlic powder, maple syrup or honey, olive oil and salt. Pour over the popcorn and thoroughly combine to ensure everything is well coated.

Serve immediately.

SIMPLE AFTERNOON TEA BISCUITS

MAKES 20-24 BISCUITS OF DIFFERENT SHAPES AND SIZES

Is there any combination more perfect than a cup of tea and a biscuit? I think not. This simple biscuit recipe ensures a dream match with your hot drink of choice – perfect for when you need a little breather. They make a great snack to serve up to mates who've popped over for a cuppa and a catch-up. They're so easy to make, so if baking isn't normally your thing, why not start off with this simple recipe to get the ball rolling?

85g unsalted butter

100g coconut palm sugar

1 egg

200g wholemeal spelt flour

½ tsp baking powder

Pinch of sea salt

Preheat the oven to 200°C/180°C fan/400°F/Gas mark 6 and line a baking tray with baking parchment.

Cream together the butter and sugar in a large bowl, then beat in the egg. Fold in the flour, baking powder and salt until the mixture comes together as a dough. Cover with cling film and refrigerate for 15 minutes.

Once chilled but still pliable, roll out the dough to a thickness of 1cm. With a cookie cutter of your choice, cut out as many biscuits as you can, then bring the remaining dough back together, roll out again and cut out the remaining biscuits.

Place on the baking tray and bake for 8–10 minutes until golden. Remove from the oven and leave to cool for 10 minutes. Transfer to a wire rack and leave to cool completely.

Store in an airtight container for up to 1 week.

AFTERNOON PICK-ME-UP GINGER CITRUS SMOOTHIE

SERVES 2

I adore ginger and the zing it adds to your day. I more often than not pop it in teas and hot drinks, but it works so well in this cooling smoothie. The fresh citrus flavours marry with the ginger beautifully, making this beyond refreshing. It will awaken your senses without sending you on a caffeine rollercoaster, and will give you a real boost for the rest of the day.

2 ripe bananas, peeled, sliced and frozen

4 seedless oranges, peeled

2 tbsp lime juice

2 tbsp lemon juice

1cm piece of root ginger, peeled and grated

Ice, to serve

Put all the ingredients, apart from the ice, in the bowl of a food processor or in a high-speed blender and blitz for a minute or two until completely smooth.

Pour into two large glasses with the ice and serve immediately.

CHOCOLATE MILK

SERVES 2

This is my favourite way to get veg into my kids. They have no idea they're slurping down a ton of spinach in this creamy, chocolatey drink. I adore this smoothie too, so I'll make a big jug of it for us all to share as a little afternoon pick-me-up. The dates make this drink just sweet enough and add a boost of fibre, and you're also getting some healthy carbs from the banana and the oat milk. Chocolate heaven!

500ml oat milk or almond milk

2 Medjool dates, pitted

½ ripe banana, peeled

1 tbsp unsweetened cocoa powder, plus a little extra for sprinkling

1 tsp vanilla extract

Large handful of spinach leaves

5 ice cubes

Small pinch of sea salt

Place all the ingredients in the bowl of a food processor or in a high-speed blender and blitz for 1 minute or until you have a smooth consistency.

Pour into glasses and serve immediately.

AFTERNOON
PICK-ME-UP
GINGER CITRUS
SMOOTHIE p112

CHOCOLATE
MILK p113

RAW CARROT & CHIA BITES

MAKES 18-20 MINI SQUARES

You may have noticed by now that there are a few carrot cake variations in this book – from the Carrot cake tray bake (page 203) to the Carrot cake porridge (page 15), I cannot get enough of the flavour combination. These raw treats are so easy to make and are packed with goodness. The chia seeds offer up some omega, the flax aids digestion and the carrot boosts your daily vitamin C intake. All natural sweetness and goodness powering up your day. Enjoy as a snack or a little sweet bite after dinner.

1 carrot, peeled and coarsely grated

2 tbsp sunflower seeds

1 tbsp nut butter (e.g. almond, peanut, cashew)

2 tbsp coconut oil, melted

1 tbsp chia seeds

12 dates, pitted

1 tsp flax seeds

1 tsp mixed spice

1 tsp ground cinnamon

40g desiccated coconut

Line a 24 x 16cm loaf tin (or any dish or Tupperware container of a similar size) with cling film.

Place all the ingredients in the bowl of a food processor and blitz until they come together when pressed between your fingers.

Scatter the desiccated coconut over the base of the tin. Place the mixture on top and gently flatten it out so that the coconut is covered. Cover and refrigerate for 30 minutes, or place in the freezer for 10.

Gently pull up the edges of the cling film to release the flattened mixture. Cut into small squares of equal size. Serve them with the desiccated coconut side upper most. Store in an airtight container in the fridge for 5 days. You can also freeze them and defrost whenever you need.

VANILLA, OATMEAL & WALNUT LOAF CAKE

SERVES 8–10

I started to use ground oats instead of flour after realising in the middle of making a cake that I had no flour in the house! They're a perfect substitute and are a very healthy alternative to use in cakes and biscuits. This loaf cake is so moist and moreish and looks beautiful with its crumble topping. The crunch on top adds a whole other level of sensation and works so well with the moist loaf beneath. The coconut palm sugar makes this bake taste really caramelly and is much easier on your system as it is not refined. A decadent afternoon treat for a little tea party, or just as lovely stored in a tin for whenever the moment strikes!

225g coconut oil or unsalted butter, at room temperature

225g coconut palm sugar

1 tsp vanilla extract

4 eggs, beaten

225g oats, ground to a powder in a food processor

2 tsp baking powder

3 tbsp milk (almond, rice or dairy)

For the topping:

40g white spelt flour

30g extra virgin coconut oil or unsalted butter

30g rolled oats

30g coconut palm sugar

30g walnuts, roughly chopped

1 tbsp honey, for drizzling

Pinch of sea salt

Preheat the oven to 180°C/160°C fan/350°F/Gas mark 4 and grease a 20 x 10cm loaf tin and line with baking parchment.

For the topping, put the spelt flour in a bowl. Rub in the coconut oil or butter until you have gravel-sized lumps. Add the oats, coconut palm sugar, walnuts and salt and mix together. Set aside.

For the loaf cake, cream together the coconut oil or butter with the sugar and vanilla extract. Beat in the eggs, oatmeal, baking powder and milk.

Transfer the mixture to the loaf tin and smooth out. Spread the oat and walnut mixture evenly over the top and bake for 50–60 minutes, until golden and firm and until a skewer inserted into the centre of the cake comes out clean. Cover with foil if it browns too quickly.

Leave it to cool completely before slicing, otherwise it will be crumbly. When you are ready to serve, drizzle over a little honey.

SOOTHING GINGER & TURMERIC TEA

MAKES 2 MUGS OF TEA

I'm a bit of a coffee addict, so I'm always looking for new hot drinks to steer me away from a caffeine overload. This soothing and comforting drink certainly does the trick as it offers a kick from the ginger plus many noted health benefits from the turmeric, which is the best natural anti-inflammatory out there. If you want to sweeten it up add a spoonful of honey or maple syrup.

1 lemon, halved

3cm piece of root ginger, peeled and sliced

¼ tsp ground turmeric

Juice one half of the lemon and slice the other half.

Add the sliced ginger to a pan together with the ground turmeric and 550ml of water and place over a high heat.

Bring to a rolling boil (a fierce boil that won't stop if you stir it), then remove from the heat immediately, add the lemon juice and leave to infuse for a few minutes.

Divide between two mugs and serve with the lemon slices.

Cooking for your family can be tricky terrain to navigate, as everyone has different desires and needs. Take my family. The six of us range from toddler to forty years old. Five eat meat; one won't eat fish; four adore bananas, two cringe at the sight of them; one is obsessed with sweetcorn, one won't even look at it; five of us love most veg, one doesn't (*cough, cough*, REX!); one prefers the healthiest version of everything, three would rather the opposite; two need coffee to survive; all love chocolate. So as you can see, it's a mixed old bag of six very different tummies and tongues.

The way my husband and I sail this stormy sea of mealtimes is by making one meal at dinnertime, but customising it to each individual's preferences where possible. Having a catalogue of meals I know work for most of the family (and for anyone else who may be dining round ours) helps to make mealtimes quicker, less 'shouty' with the little guys and delicious for everyone. Tummies get filled, mouths smile and time isn't wasted.

One recipe everyone in my family is happy to devour is the Coconut-crusted haddock fingers on page 135. Yes, Rex may slather them with ketchup but I can live with that as I know he is getting some fresh protein from the haddock which will help his brain and continuing growth. I'll make the Sweet potato pasta salad (page 145) for Jesse and I can then use up leftover sweet potato for creamy mash for Honey (her absolute fave). If my folks are over for lunch or dinner I love to make simple, quick and easy tray bakes (pages 130 and 140). It's such a joy to throw a random assortment of vibrant veg into a baking tray and roast them until they're sweet and tender. I could happily live off that sort of meal. It feels hearty and wholesome and you know all of those magical vegetables are doing your system so much good.

One dish that everyone in our house asks for regularly is pizza. It's a winner with the kids as they can easily get involved with the cooking part. Most days I try and pin down Rex's short concentration span to cook or bake with me. Knowing he gets to eat the results is usually a good incentive, and seems to make him slightly more lenient in trying new foods. It's rarely easy with small kids but I think if you just keep trying then one day they'll pick up that previously detested food and give it a whirl! The Quick & healthy pizza (page 132) is fun to make, versatile and delicious.

My kitchen is chaos after I've cooked for the family. It peaks in decibels, it can be frustrating at times but it is mostly joyful and a lot of fun. I hope these dishes warm the hearts and tummies in your own home.

FAMILY
FAVOURITES

JESSE'S FISH SARNIE

SERVES 2

This is my husband's dream lunch. Serve this up to a loved one and they will swoon with delight. It's the perfect lunch if you're ravenous after a long, blustery walk and should be chomped up with vigour. There's a ton of protein in this recipe from the haddock, loads of freshness from the lettuce and avocado, and plenty of flavour from the zesty lemon and the punchy mustard. Jesse adds a ton of hot sauce to his to give it a real kick, but splash it on or not as you desire.

2 skinless and boneless haddock fillets

Grated zest of 1 unwaxed lemon

2 tsp olive oil

2 spelt or gluten-free burger buns

Hummus (page 49, or shop-bought)

2 tsp wholegrain mustard

Small handful of lettuce or rocket leaves

1 avocado, halved, stone removed and flesh sliced

2 tsp hot sauce, like Tabasco (optional)

Sea salt and freshly ground black pepper

Season the haddock fillets on both sides with the lemon zest and salt and pepper. Add the oil to a pan and place over a medium heat. Fry the fillets for 3–4 minutes on each side, until golden and cooked through.

Cut the buns in half and spread the bottom halves with hummus and the top halves with wholegrain mustard. Place the lettuce or rocket on top of the hummus and layer the avocado on top of that. Position the haddock on top of the avocado and drizzle over a little of the hot sauce, if using. Cover with the top half of the bun and serve immediately.

HEALING VEGAN STEW

SERVES 4

After writing my first cookbook, Cook Happy, Cook Healthy, I got a lot of lovely feedback about the vegan recipes I included, so I wanted to include a few more in my second book. This stew is very hearty and is flavour-packed and full of goodness. There are the anti-inflammatory benefits of the turmeric and ginger and all the vibrant nutrients exploding from the kidney beans and the kale. It's colourful, delicious and filling: a rainbow in a bowl!

2 tbsp olive oil

1 carrot, peeled and diced

1 onion, diced

1 clove garlic, crushed

1 tsp ground cinnamon

½ tsp ground ginger

½ tsp ground turmeric (optional)

300g passata

1 large sweet potato, diced (no need to peel)

425g tin kidney beans

50g quinoa

1 litre vegetable stock

100g kale, rinsed and dried, tough stems removed, and roughly chopped

Sourdough or spelt bread, to serve

Sea salt and freshly ground pepper

Heat the oil in a pan. Add the carrot and onion and sauté for 5 minutes over a medium heat. Add the garlic, cinnamon, ginger, turmeric (if using) and a large pinch of salt and pepper and fry for another minute or two until fragrant.

Add the passata and simmer for 5 minutes. Add the sweet potato, kidney beans, quinoa and stock, bring to the boil, then reduce the heat and simmer gently for 20 minutes until the sweet potato and quinoa are almost cooked. Add the kale and cook for another 5 minutes. Season well to taste.

Serve with a large chunk of bread to dip in.

BAKED COD, AUBERGINE & TOMATOES

SERVES 4

When I was out at dinner with some mates recently, one of them ordered (and devoured) a tasty-looking dish of fish wrapped in bacon. It looked so succulent and pretty, so I got to work devising a pescatarian version. Aubergine works well as a substitute for bacon as it wraps well and gives the fish a delicious smokey flavour. This is a pretty easy dinner to make and doesn't take long at all. Serve it with a baked sweet potato or salad. Bliss.

1 aubergine, cut lengthways into ¼cm-thin strips
4 tbsp olive oil
4 boneless cod fillets, skin on
Grated zest of 1 unwaxed lemon
1 tsp smoked paprika
250g cherry tomatoes
Sea salt and freshly ground black pepper

Preheat the oven to 200°C/180°C fan/400°F/Gas mark 6 and line a baking sheet with baking parchment.

Brush the 4 longest slices of aubergine on both sides with half the olive oil. Keep any remaining aubergine to use as an extra ingredient in a simple vegetable tray bake (page 130).

Place the aubergine in a pan set over a medium heat and cook for 3 minutes on each side until slightly softened and golden, but not completely cooked through.

Season the aubergine and cod with salt and pepper and most of the lemon zest and smoked paprika. Gently wrap a slice of aubergine around each of the cod fillets, positioning them on the baking tray with the ends of the aubergine tucked in underneath the base of the fillet. Use a cocktail stick to secure in place if necessary.

Add the tomatoes, sprinkle over the remaining zest and smoked paprika and drizzle over the remaining 2 tablespoons of olive oil. Place in the oven and bake for 20 minutes, until the fish and aubergine are cooked through and the tomatoes have burst open, releasing their juices.

Remove from the oven and serve immediately.

SUPER-SIMPLE VEGGIE TRAY BAKE

SERVES 4 AS A SIDE DISH

If you're feeling run down, or you simply haven't found the time to get your five a day recently, this recipe is the one for you. It's a one-stop shop for all the vitamins and nutrients you need and it tastes divine. I love that you can just throw a bunch of fresh ingredients into the oven and take out a tasty dish. I have recently got into roasting avocado, as I love how it slightly alters the flavour and texture. Baked feta is one of life's small delights too, adding such creaminess and warmth to this dish. Eat this for dinner as it is, or have it as a side with the Sticky smoked paprika and maple chicken wings (page 167) if you have meat-eating friends round.

8 large plum tomatoes, halved

1 courgette, roughly chopped

1 pepper, deseeded and sliced

100g feta, broken into chunks

1 avocado, halved, stone removed and flesh sliced

Handful of rosemary sprigs

2 tbsp olive oil

3 tbsp pine nuts

Sea salt and freshly ground black pepper

Preheat the oven to 200°C/180°C fan/400°F/Gas mark 6.

Place the tomatoes, courgette, pepper, feta, avocado and rosemary on a baking tray, drizzle over the olive oil and season well with salt and pepper. Toss to combine then bake for 15 minutes.

Scatter over the pine nuts and bake for another 5–10 minutes until everything is golden and delicious. Serve immediately.

BAKED CABBAGE & APPLE

SERVES 6-8 AS A SIDE DISH

Every year my mum makes a huge dish of this for Christmas dinner and for the food-frenzied days that follow. It works really well with a big feast, but it's also a perfect side dish for dinner, such as the Sea bass with beetroot and horseradish (page 162), and any leftovers are great in sandwiches or used as a top-up for a salad. I adore the Christmassy spices and punch in this dish. Each time you take a mouthful you get a hit of new flavours. It takes a while to bake, so make sure you get it in the oven in plenty of time if you're planning on serving it with something else.

1 red cabbage, shredded

2 medium apples, cored and chopped into 1cm chunks

2 sticks of celery, thinly sliced

4 tbsp olive oil

4 tbsp apple cider vinegar

2 tbsp coconut palm sugar

½ tsp ground cloves

1 tsp ground cinnamon

1 tsp ground nutmeg

Sea salt and freshly ground black pepper

Preheat the oven to 180°C/160°C fan/350°F/Gas mark 4.

Combine all of the ingredients in a bowl. Season with two teaspoons of salt and a good grinding of pepper. Taste and adjust the seasoning if necessary.

Transfer the mixture to a medium casserole dish and bake for 1 hour and 45 minutes, until it has reduced down and cooked through. Taste, and if necessary, adjust the seasoning with a little more salt and nutmeg.

QUICK & HEALTHY PIZZA

SERVES 2

Making your own pizza from scratch is so satisfying. My kids love to help out too, which I'm all for as they get to see what is going into their meals – and also it's just a whole heap of fun. The spelt flour has a lot less gluten than normal flour, so is easier on your system, and the toppings are fresh and health-boosting. Making your own dough needn't be fiddly or laborious, as you'll see from this recipe. The pesto gives this recipe a very moreish flavour and marries so well with the cheese. The beauty of making pizza for your friends or family is that they can customise their own to their heart's content. The perfect social feeding frenzy for all to enjoy!

For the dough:

150g white spelt flour, plus extra for dusting

100g wholegrain spelt flour

7g sachet of fast-action yeast

1 tsp honey

160ml warm water

1 tsp fine sea salt

For the toppings:

4 tbsp pesto (page 150 or shop-bought)

1 ball of buffalo mozzarella, torn into pieces

Handful of cherry tomatoes, halved

Handful of rocket leaves

1 tsp dried chilli flakes (optional)

Extra virgin olive oil, for drizzling

To make the dough, put the flours, yeast and salt in the bowl of a stand mixer fitted with a dough hook and stir to combine. Add the honey and water, then switch on the machine and knead for 3 minutes until it comes together into a ball of dough. Alternatively you can knead by hand for about 6 minutes until smooth and springy.

Remove the dough and divide in half. Roll out each ball on a lightly floured surface to a round measuring about 18cm. Transfer the pizza bases to two lightly oiled baking sheets and set aside to rise while you prepare your toppings.

Preheat the oven to 240°C/220°C fan/475°F/Gas mark 9.

After 20 minutes, spread the pesto over the pizza bases. Lay the mozzarella and tomatoes on top and bake for 10–12 minutes until crisp.

Remove from the oven and top with the rocket leaves, scatter over the dried chilli flakes (if using) and drizzle over a little extra virgin olive oil. Serve immediately.

COCONUT-CRUSTED HADDOCK FINGERS
& MUSHY PEAS

SERVES 4

I love making fish fingers for the whole family since every member will eat them with little complaint. I'm always looking for new ways to make them and the coconut in this recipe gives this classic a whole new twist, as it gives the fish a slightly sweetened note and even more crunch. Mushy peas are one of my all-time favourite foods, so I'm happy to dollop a large portion of them next to this sublime fish dish. This whole meal takes no time at all to make. Whip it up and enjoy every bite!

400g frozen peas

Small handful of fresh flat-leaf parsley leaves, finely chopped, plus extra to serve

Grated zest of ½ unwaxed lemon

2 tbsp extra virgin olive oil

60g fresh breadcrumbs, gluten-free if you prefer

4 tbsp desiccated coconut

100g rice flour or corn flour

2 eggs, beaten

500g skinless and boneless haddock fillet

4 tbsp coconut oil or sunflower oil

1 lemon, cut into wedges, to serve

Mayonnaise, to serve

Extra virgin olive oil, for drizzling (optional)

Sea salt and freshly ground black pepper

Add the peas to a pan of boiling water and cook for 4 minutes until completely tender. Drain the peas, then add them to a bowl together with the parsley, lemon zest and olive oil. Combine and roughly mash the peas with a fork (or use a food processor). Season to taste with salt and pepper. Keep warm.

Combine the breadcrumbs with the desiccated coconut and 1 teaspoon each of salt and pepper.

Cut the haddock into 16 2 x 7cm fingers. Coat each finger in the flour, then dip into the beaten egg and finally roll in the breadcrumb mixture until evenly covered on all sides. Set aside on a plate while you finish the rest.

Add the coconut oil or sunflower oil to a pan and place over a medium heat. Add the haddock fingers and fry for 2–3 minutes on each side, or until crisp, golden and cooked through.

Divide the mushy peas between the plates, top with the fish fingers, scatter over some parsley and drizzle over a little extra virgin olive oil, if you like. Serve immediately with the lemon wedges and mayonnaise to dunk into.

ASIAN FRIED RICE
WITH TIGER PRAWNS

SERVES 4

We often have a lot of leftover rice in our house from the kids' dinnertimes so I'll store it in the fridge to use the following day in this dish. It holds together really well when the rice has been in the fridge overnight, but that's by no means necessary, so cook from scratch there and then if you don't have leftovers. My stepkids adore this dish as they're big prawn fans, but it's also glorious without if you want a veggie dish. The flavours are sensational and moreish and make this such a comforting dish. Get all the ingredients prepped before you start cooking, as you need to throw them all into the pan quite quickly.

3 tbsp vegetable oil

350g tiger prawns, peeled

6 cloves garlic, crushed

2 eggs, beaten

4cm piece of root ginger, peeled and finely grated

2 tbsp tamari or soy sauce

½ tsp toasted sesame oil

2 tsp rice vinegar

1 tbsp lime juice

1 red chilli, deseeded and thinly sliced

800g cooked jasmine rice (roughly 370g uncooked)

4 spring onions, finely sliced

1 red onion, halved and very thinly sliced

Small handful of fresh Thai or regular basil leaves, to serve

Sea salt and freshly ground black pepper

Pour 1 tablespoon of the vegetable oil into a large wok or pan and set over a high heat. When it is hot, add the prawns and stir-fry for 2 minutes, then add a quarter of the garlic and stir-fry for another minute, just until the prawns are cooked through. Season with salt and pepper and remove to a bowl.

Add the remaining 2 tablespoons of oil to the pan. Once hot, add the beaten eggs and scramble for 30 seconds until just cooked. Add the ginger, tamari or soy sauce, sesame oil, rice vinegar, lime juice, most of the chilli and the remaining garlic and stir-fry for another 30 seconds. Add the cooked rice and toss together, then spread the rice out over the base of the pan. Fry for 30 seconds then toss together. Repeat this process a few more times until the rice begins to crisp up. This may take a little longer with freshly cooked rice as it contains more moisture.

Add most of the spring onions and red onion and toss together. Adjust the seasoning to taste (don't use soy sauce as this will make the rice soggy).

Serve immediately on a large plate with the cooked prawns, the basil and the remaining chilli, spring onion and red onion scattered over.

PARADISE CHICKEN CURRY

SERVES 4

Once, while on holiday with one of my close friends, I took an afternoon cooking course. The first dish we tackled was a chicken curry made with fresh local ingredients. Bliss! This curry is inspired by that cooking lesson many moons ago and has been enjoyed by many people, my stepchildren especially. They are chicken curry experts and are very honest, so I was chuffed when this dish got a firm thumbs up. It's full of spice and exotic flavours and has a ton of health-boosting protein from the chicken. If like me you don't eat chicken, just substitute it for smoked tofu. The flavours and textures work just as well.

30g coconut oil

2 onions, thinly sliced

4 cloves garlic, thinly sliced

10g root ginger, peeled and thinly sliced

2 tbsp red curry paste

1 tsp dried chilli flakes

1 tbsp ground turmeric

1 tsp ground cumin

10 cardamom pods, bruised with a rolling pin so the skin pops open

5 cloves

4 tbsp tomato purée

400g tin coconut milk

1kg skinless, boneless chicken thighs, chopped into bite-size chunks

150g spinach

Cooked brown rice or quinoa, to serve

Small handful of chives or fresh coriander leaves, to serve

Sea salt

Put the coconut oil in a large high-sided pan and set over a medium heat. Add the onions and sauté for 8 minutes until slightly softened. Add the garlic and ginger and continue to sweat down for another 2 minutes until aromatic.

Add the curry paste, chilli flakes, turmeric, cumin, cardamoms, cloves and tomato purée and fry for 2 minutes to release the flavour of the spices.

Stir the coconut milk into the spice paste until combined. Add the chicken, 200ml of water and a pinch of salt. Bring to the boil, then reduce the heat to low and simmer for 20–25 minutes until the chicken is cooked through. Stir in the spinach and cook for a minute or two until it wilts down. Taste and adjust the seasoning if necessary.

Serve in bowls with rice or quinoa, scattered with the chives or coriander.

FLEXI OPTION

I'm doing this the other way round on this recipe! If you'd like a veggie alternative for this meaty dish, just substitute the chicken for cubes of smoked tofu and cook the same way.

SALMON TRAY BAKE

SERVES 4

I love a tray bake as you get to whack a whole host of foods and flavours together, which makes it quick to make and also extremely flavoursome. Each ingredient seeps into the next, complementing each other and adding to the overall deliciousness. This is a very simple and easy recipe but will feed four hungry faces very well indeed. It is a good-looking, no-messing dish that is bursting with great protein and healthy veg!

650g new potatoes

3 tbsp olive oil

16 asparagus spears

1 red onion, cut into wedges

250g cherry tomatoes

2 fresh rosemary sprigs

2 tbsp balsamic vinegar

4 boneless salmon fillets, skin on

Sea salt and freshly ground black pepper

Preheat the oven to 200°C/180°C fan/400°F/Gas mark 6.

Put the potatoes and oil in a baking tray and toss to combine. Season well with salt and pepper and bake for 15 minutes until slightly golden. Add the onion, tomatoes, rosemary and balsamic vinegar, combine, and bake for another 10 minutes.

Season the salmon fillets and add to the tray of vegetables together with the asparagus and cook for a final 10–12 minutes, until the salmon is just cooked.

Serve immediately.

SQUASH, CARROT & CUCUMBER RISOTTO

SERVES 4–6

I haven't eaten meat since I was around ten years old, so many's the time I've been at a restaurant or a dinner party and been served the obvious vegetarian option of risotto. It's usually very gloopy and heavy and I can feel it sticking to the sides of my stomach with every bite. This is the perfect antidote to that: a lighter, dairy-free option that is fresh and delicious. The short-grain rice absorbs the stock, which gives it a creamy texture without adding vast quantities of cheese to the mix, and the cucumber offers a lovely crunch to finish off proceedings.

2 tbsp olive oil

1 red onion, diced

125g raw unsalted cashew nuts

2 carrots, peeled and diced

1 leek, trimmed and finely sliced

400g butternut squash, peeled, deseeded and diced

4 cloves garlic, crushed

320g short-grain brown rice

900ml vegetable stock

1 tbsp tamari or soy sauce

½ cucumber, halved lengthways and sliced

1 ripe avocado, stone removed, peeled and flesh sliced

Handful of lamb's lettuce or rocket, to serve

Sea salt and freshly ground black pepper

Add the oil to a pan (with a lid) and set over a medium heat. Add the onion, cashew nuts, carrots, leek and squash and sauté for 12 minutes until the onions are softened and translucent. Add the garlic and fry for a further 2 minutes until aromatic.

Add the rice and fry for 4 minutes, stirring it into the vegetables. Add the vegetable stock, tamari or soy sauce, half a teaspoon of salt and a grinding of pepper (if you are using instant stock you may not need to add extra salt).

Bring to the boil and simmer vigorously for 5 minutes, stirring now and again. Reduce the heat to low, add the cucumber, put the lid on and simmer gently for 45–50 minutes, stirring now and again, until the rice has absorbed all of the liquid. Taste and adjust the seasoning if necessary with a little more salt or tamari or soy sauce.

Serve in bowls with the sliced avocado and salad leaves on top.

SWEET POTATO PASTA SALAD

SERVES 4

This is a wonderfully easy dinner to make for the family or for a group of mates and takes no time at all. My love for sweet potato continues in this recipe, as it adds so much flavour and depth to this pasta dish. The roasted red peppers and spinach are colourful, restorative and nutrient-packed, and the balsamic vinegar gives it a nice kick! Use whatever pasta you like: gluten-free or wholewheat work really well, but go with your own personal fave!

800g sweet potato, peeled and chopped into bite-size pieces

2 tbsp olive oil

400g wholewheat fusilli

1 ball of buffalo mozzarella, torn into pieces

100g roasted red peppers from a jar, sliced

100g baby spinach leaves

60g pecan nuts, roasted

3 tbsp extra virgin olive oil

3 tbsp balsamic vinegar

Sea salt and freshly ground black pepper

Preheat the oven to 200°C/180°C fan/400°F/Gas mark 6.

Put the sweet potato in a baking tray and toss with the olive oil. Season well with salt and pepper and bake in the oven for 20–25 minutes until tender.

Cook the pasta in a large pan of salted boiling water as per the packet instructions, or until al dente. Drain well.

Combine the pasta with the sweet potato, mozzarella, red peppers, spinach, pecan nuts, extra virgin olive oil and balsamic vinegar. Taste and adjust the seasoning if necessary.

Serve immediately.

FLEXI OPTION

If you eat fish, you could add to the finished dish about 300g of smoked mackerel, torn into bite size chunks.

ROAST BUTTERNUT SQUASH
WITH CREAMY LEEKS

SERVES 4

When we were in Ibiza last summer, my friend Nick made us the most incredible dish of butternut squash and creamy leeks. I couldn't stop eating it or thinking about it afterwards. I try not to eat too much heavy dairy as it sometimes gives me a sore tummy, and this recipe had a heap of cream in it, so I set to work making a dairy-free version. The coconut cream when reduced down acts like a full-fat cream but without the dairy. This might be my all-time favourite way to cook leeks. They become even sweeter and juicier and are dreamy on top of the roasted squash. This is a really nice lunch if you have the time to make it, or a perfect dinnertime side dish or serving platter for all to get stuck in to.

2 small butternut squash, halved lengthways and deseeded

2 tbsp olive oil

2 tbsp coconut oil, or more olive oil

4 leeks, trimmed and finely sliced

4 garlic cloves, crushed

100g coconut cream

2 tbsp toasted pine nuts

Small handful of fresh flat-leaf parsley leaves, roughly chopped

Sea salt and freshly ground black pepper

Preheat the oven to 200°C/180°C fan/400°F/Gas mark 6.

Cut each half of squash lengthways into 3 pieces. Transfer to a baking tray, coat with the olive oil and season well with salt and pepper. Bake for 30–35 minutes until tender.

Put the coconut oil or extra olive oil in a pan and set over a medium heat. Add the leeks and sweat down for 10 minutes, taking care not to let them burn. Add the garlic and sauté for another 2 minutes. Add the coconut cream and simmer for 20 minutes, until it has reduced down and become thick and creamy. Season to taste.

Divide the creamy leeks between 4 plates, position the lengths of squash on top of the leeks and scatter over the pine nuts and parsley. Serve immediately.

Food can be such a healing wonder. The practice of sitting down with friends, taking a hiatus from everything else consuming your life and engaging with others . . . Bliss. Food has the power to do this every day. What a joy! I love nothing more than packing my kitchen with an eclectic mix of people, getting out some big serving platters and bowls, piling them with food and then letting everyone get stuck in. It's much less formal than sitting at a designated place at the table with a plate of food. And it's easier for me as people can help themselves to what they like whilst the conversation flows. Everyone is welcome to go back for seconds, thirds or just keep grazing. Leftovers can be stored and eaten the next day or reinvented into a completely new dish. What's not to love?

Back in my twenties, when faced with multiple humans at my house, I would have called up my local pizza place and got them to deliver some life-saving boxes of their finest stuffed crust. I would have panicked at the thought of having to feed anyone but me. The pressure of knowing what others like and making enough for everyone was horrible. These days I relish getting a mixed bunch together to try out my food. I love the feedback; it keeps me experimenting to get dishes tasting as scrummy as they can possibly be – and it tops up my inherent need to nurture.

I love feeding and comforting whoever sets foot in my house and making sure I pack them off at the end with a doggy bag of leftovers, or at the very least a sliver of cake.

I now know that feeding a group doesn't have to be daunting at all. You don't need to keep an eye on five different things cooking with a spreadsheet of timings. You can instead, quite easily, lovingly rustle up some fantastic dishes that everyone can dive into. If you have meat-eaters and veggies coming over to eat, then the Spicy moroccan veggie burgers (page 164) and the Sticky smoked paprika & maple chicken wings (page 167) are both excellent options.

The Smokey cauliflower (page 152) is an enticing side dish (and any leftovers can double up as a perfect portion to beef up a packed lunch the next day), and the little Parsnip rostis (page 156) look impressive but are easy to make and are packed with flavour. They work as a perfect starter or a little side dish to a heartier main.

Make life easy for yourself and enjoy the cooking experience when your house is more occupied than usual. Sharing is caring and all that!

FOOD TO SHARE

BAKED AUBERGINE

WITH BROWN RICE & PESTO

SERVES 4

This dish is a warming treasure trove of flavours. The aubergine, when baked, oozes with natural juices and flavours, which complement the rice, vegetables and feta cheese. My tummy is rumbling just thinking about it! The homemade pesto sits beautifully atop this dish, giving it a richness and an added boost of flavour. Serve with a side salad or with the Fried asparagus and courgette chip salad (page 87).

2 aubergines, halved lengthways

3 tbsp olive oil

150g brown rice

1 carrot, peeled and diced

1 leek, trimmed and finely chopped

3 cloves garlic, crushed

80g feta, crumbled (optional)

2 tbsp flaked almonds, toasted, to serve

Sea salt and freshly ground black pepper

For the pesto:

40g raw unsalted cashew nuts

40g fresh basil leaves

1 clove garlic

1 tbsp nutritional yeast or grated Parmesan

¼ tsp sea salt

100ml extra virgin olive oil

Preheat the oven to 200°C/180°C fan/400°F/Gas mark 6.

Score the flesh of the aubergines, brush with 2 tablespoons of the oil, season well and bake in the oven for 35–40 minutes until soft and golden.

To make the pesto, place the cashew nuts on a baking tray and bake for 5–7 minutes until golden. Remove from the oven and allow to cool, then add to the bowl of a food processor with the basil, garlic, nutritional yeast or grated Parmesan and salt. Blitz until very finely chopped, then drizzle in the oil until you have a thick pesto. Set to one side.

In a saucepan (with a lid) bring the brown rice to the boil in a little over double its quantity of salted water. Reduce the heat and simmer for 40–50 minutes until the brown rice is tender but still chewy. Drain well and leave to one side.

Add the remaining tablespoon of oil to a pan and set over a medium–high heat. Add the carrot and leek and sauté for 10 minutes until slightly softened. Add the garlic and fry for another minute or two until aromatic, taking care not to let it burn.

Once the aubergines are cooked, remove from the oven and scoop out the flesh, taking care not to tear the skin of the aubergine. Put the flesh in a bowl and combine with the brown rice and vegetables. Season to taste.

Divide the mixture between the 4 aubergine skins (any that's left over can be served alongside). Drizzle over the pesto and top with the crumbled feta (if using) and the flaked almonds. Serve immediately.

SMOKEY CAULIFLOWER

SERVES 2-3 AS A SIDE DISH

The smokey flavours of the spices in this recipe really bring the cauliflower to life. I could eat heaps of this in one sitting, but it is a great little side dish if you are feeding a gang of friends. It's quick and easy to make, and will completely wipe out any memories of your nan boiling the life out of this humble veg.

2 tbsp olive oil

1 head of cauliflower, cut into florets

1 tsp ground cumin

1 tsp smoked paprika

2 cloves garlic, sliced

1 tbsp fresh flat-leaf parsley leaves, chopped, to serve

Sea salt and freshly ground black pepper

Put the oil in a pan and set over a medium heat. Add the cauliflower florets and fry for 5 minutes, stirring now and again.

Add the cumin and paprika and season with half a teaspoon of salt and a grinding of pepper. Fry for another 5 minutes until golden and slightly charred in places. Add the sliced garlic and fry for another minute or two until aromatic, taking care not to let it burn.

Serve in a bowl with the parsley scattered over.

COURGETTE BALLS
& CARROT NOODLES

MAKES 25 SMALL
COURGETTE BALLS,
SERVES 4

This recipe mimics the classic spaghetti and meatballs dish but is almost entirely made up of veg, with a little bit of protein for good measure. It's a wonderful and fun way to get your five a day in one hit as you're getting such a good portion of courgette and carrot, along with the protein from the mozarella and the almonds. The tart tamari dressing tops this super dish off perfectly.

450g courgettes, coarsely grated
½ onion, very finely chopped
50g ground almonds
2 eggs, beaten
80g mozzarella, chopped
Grated zest of ½ unwaxed lemon
2 cloves garlic, crushed
2 tsp toasted sesame seeds, plus extra to serve
1 tsp ground coriander
Small handful of fresh flat-leaf parsley leaves, finely chopped
4 tbsp olive oil
3 large carrots, peeled and ends removed
1 tbsp tamari
1 tsp toasted sesame oil
1 spring onion, finely chopped
Sea salt and freshly ground black pepper

Spread the grated courgette out on a board and sprinkle over 1 teaspoon of salt. Leave to one side for 10 minutes to degorge.

Meanwhile, in a large bowl combine the onion, ground almonds, eggs, mozzarella, lemon zest, garlic, sesame seeds, ground coriander, most of the parsley and a grind of pepper.

Place the courgettes in a clean tea towel and squeeze out as much liquid as possible. Add this to the mozzarella mixture, and mix together until thoroughly combined. One tablespoon at a time, shape the mixture into balls of equal size, measuring about 2.5cm.

Put 3 tablespoons of the olive oil in a pan over a medium heat. Once hot, gently add the courgette balls. Fry for 5–6 minutes, moving them around now and again so they are crisp and golden on all sides. Remove and keep warm.

Spiralise the carrots then add to a pan with the remaining tablespoon of olive oil and set over a low–medium heat. Sauté gently for 4–5 minutes until the carrot noodles have softened slightly. Mix in the tamari, sesame oil and most of the spring onions and stir to combine.

Plate up the carrots and top with the courgette balls, the remaining spring onions and the sesame seeds. Serve immediately.

COURGETTE
BALLS &
CARROT
NOODLES
p153

SMOKEY
CAULIFLOWER
p152

PARSNIP ROSTIS
WITH A BROAD
BEAN & MINT
TOPPING p156

BUTTERNUT
SQUASH RINGS
WITH QUINOA &
RED PEPPER p157

PARSNIP ROSTIS
WITH A BROAD BEAN & MINT TOPPING

MAKES 8-10 ROSTIS,
SERVES 4

My lovely husband took me out for a delicious meal for our second wedding anniversary, and one of the starters was a little like this. The broad beans and mint were grown at the restaurant we were eating at, and I promised myself I would start to grow my own the very next day. That is yet to happen! But instead I have rustled up a very similar-tasting dish to the one I gorged on that dreamy evening. The parsnips are so sweet in flavour and marry so well with the broad beans and zingy mint. I adore this dish as a starter or as a side dish. It can easily be made vegan too, by ditching the eggs and upping the flour and using nutritional yeast instead of Parmesan. Divine!

400g frozen broad beans

Small handful of fresh mint leaves, finely chopped

Grated zest of ½ unwaxed lemon

4 tbsp extra virgin olive oil, plus extra for drizzling

4 large parsnips, peeled and coarsely grated

2 eggs, beaten

4 tsp cornflour

1 tsp ground cumin

4 tbsp Parmesan cheese, finely grated, or nutritional yeast, plus extra to serve

2 tbsp coconut oil or olive oil

4 poached eggs, to serve (optional)

Dried chilli flakes, to serve (optional)

Sea salt and freshly ground black pepper

Add the broad beans to a pan of boiling water and cook for 4 minutes until completely tender. Drain and remove the outer skin to reveal the bright green inner bean. Add them to a bowl with the mint, lemon zest and olive oil. Combine and lightly mash with a fork, leaving some of the beans intact. Season to taste with salt and pepper.

Roughly chop the grated parsnip on a board. In a bowl, combine the parsnips, eggs, cornflour, cumin and Parmesan cheese. Season with half a teaspoon of salt and a grinding of pepper. Put the oil in a pan and set over a medium heat. Take 2 heaped tablespoons of the parsnip mixture and bring together into a ball. Carefully transfer the rosti to the pan and with the back of a spoon shape it into a neat disc, roughly 10cm across. The mixture will seem very loose and crumbly at this point: this is normal. Once you position it in the pan and the flour, egg and Parmesan begin to cook, the rosti will firm up and bind together. Fry for 3–4 minutes on each side, over a low–medium heat, until crisp and golden. Do the same with the rest of the mixture, so you have 8 rostis in total.

To serve, stack 2 rostis per person on a plate and top with the broad bean mixture and a poached egg, if you like. Grate over a little more Parmesan and a sprinkle of dried chilli (if using), and drizzle with a little extra virgin olive oil.

BUTTERNUT SQUASH RINGS

WITH QUINOA & RED PEPPER

SERVES 4

This pretty dish is full of dreamy flavours and will give you a ton of energy instead of making you feel heavy and lethargic. The glistening pomegranate gives this recipe loads of flavour and freshness, and the quinoa gives you a wonderful source of protein and fibre. It's the perfect serving dish for your family and friends to help themselves to!

300g quinoa, rinsed

1 small butternut squash, deseeded and cut into 1cm slices (no need to peel)

2.5 tbsp olive oil

1 red pepper, deseeded and chopped

80g kale, woody stalks removed and roughly chopped

2 corn on the cob, or 150g sweetcorn, drained and rinsed

Handful of flat leaf parsley leaves, roughly chopped

5 tbsp of the Smoked paprika tahini dressing (page 75)

2tbsp pomegranate seeds, to scatter over

Sea salt and pepper

Preheat the oven to 200°C / 180°C fan / gas mark 6.

Cut the squash widthways into 1cm thick slices. Remove the seeds from the rings and leave them intact. Roughly chop the remaining slices. Put the squash on a baking tray, toss with the olive oil and season with salt and pepper. Bake in the oven for 20–25 minutes until golden and cooked through.

Meanwhile, in a saucepan (with a lid), bring the quinoa to a boil in double its quantity of salted water. Once it has come to the boil, reduce the heat to low, keep the lid on top and cook for about 12 minutes until all the water has been absorbed. Leave to one side.

Heat the coconut oil in a pan over a medium-high heat. Add in the red pepper and stir-fry for 5 minutes until softened and slightly charred. Add in the garlic and fry for another minute until aromatic, taking care not to let it burn.

Add most of the red pepper, garlic and the chopped squash (not the rings) to the quinoa and stir to combine. Taste and adjust the seasoning if necessary.

Plate up the rings of squash and pile the quinoa on top of the rings. Top with the remaining red pepper and garlic, and scatter over the pomegranate seeds and parsley. Drizzle over a little extra virgin olive oil and balsamic vinegar and serve immediately.

ROAST CHICKEN, CASHEW & CHILLI SALAD

SERVES 4

My husband and stepkids love chicken, so we often have roast chicken leftovers begging to be made into a salad or a sandwich the following day. This salad is so quick and easy to make if you have leftovers, but if there's no chicken going spare in the fridge then you can roast the thighs on the day. I don't eat chicken but I have it on good authority from my loved ones that this is a winner!

For the roast chicken:
4 chicken thighs, skin on
2 tsp five-spice powder
2 tbsp soy sauce
1 tbsp honey
Sea salt and freshly ground black pepper

For the salad:
½ tsp dried chilli flakes, plus more to serve (optional)
2 tbsp soy sauce
1 tbsp lime juice
1 tbsp coconut palm sugar, maple syrup or honey
1 clove garlic, crushed
3cm piece of root ginger, peeled and finely grated
1 red onion, halved and thinly sliced
100g mixed leaves
20g fresh mint leaves, torn
60g roasted cashew nuts

Preheat the oven to 200°C/180°C fan/400°F/Gas mark 6.

Put the chicken thighs in a roasting tray and toss together with the five-spice powder, soy sauce and honey. Season well with salt and pepper and roast for 25–30 minutes until the skin is golden and the chicken is cooked through. Remove from the oven, cover in foil and leave to rest for 20 minutes.

Meanwhile, combine the chilli flakes, soy sauce, lime juice, sugar, honey or maple syrup, garlic and ginger in a large bowl.

Cut the chicken off the bones and tear or shred into bite-size pieces. Add the chicken pieces and red onion to the bowl of soy sauce dressing and toss together until everything is well coated.

Plate up the mixed leaves on a serving platter, top with the chicken, mint, cashew nuts and a little more of the dried chilli, if you like.

RED ONION & CAULIFLOWER TART

SERVES 8–10

Cauliflower mash is one of my favourite winter comfort foods, so I'm always experimenting with new ways of using it. This pie was a complete fluke, as I had never used cauliflower mash as a filling in this way before. It works perfectly, however, as it's creamy yet sturdy enough to hold the beautiful, caramelised onions. The pastry is really tasty, but if you prefer you can swap the butter for the same quantity of coconut oil. If you do this you'll find the pastry is more brittle, so make sure to roll it out between floured cling film, and patch up any cracks that appear when you transfer it to the tin by squeezing the pastry together.

For the pastry:

250g white spelt flour

125g unsalted butter, chilled and cut into small pieces

½ tsp fine sea salt

1 egg, beaten

For the filling:

4 red onions, sliced into 1cm wedges

2 tsp fresh thyme leaves, plus extra to serve

6 tbsp olive oil

1 tbsp honey or maple syrup

2 small heads of cauliflower (about 1kg) stalks removed and cut into small florets

4 cloves garlic, crushed

2 tbsp coconut cream, taken from the top of a tin of full-fat coconut milk

2 tbsp grated Parmesan cheese, or nutritional yeast

Sea salt and freshly ground black pepper

Preheat the oven to 200°C/180°C fan/400°F/Gas mark 6 and grease a 24cm round tart tin.

To make the pastry, put the ingredients (apart from the egg) in the bowl of a food processor and blitz until it resembles fine breadcrumbs. Add 2½–3 tablespoons of water and bring the dough together with your hands until it's a smooth ball. Flatten out into a disc, wrap in cling film and refrigerate for 20–30 minutes until chilled but still pliable. Roll out the pastry and line the tart tin with it. Cover and refrigerate for 15 minutes, then prick the base all over with a fork, line with baking parchment, fill with dry rice or baking beans and bake for 20 minutes. Remove the paper and rice or beans, brush the tart with the beaten egg and bake for 5 minutes until the tart shell is dry and biscuity. Leave the oven on.

Toss the onions with the thyme and 2 tablespoons of the oil, season well with salt and pepper and bake in the oven for 10 minutes. Drizzle over the honey or maple syrup and cook for another 10–15 minutes until soft and caramelised.

Place the remaining oil and cauliflower in a large pan (with a lid) and fry for 2 minutes over a medium–high heat. Turn the heat to low, add 7 tablespoons of water, put the lid on and steam for 20 minutes. Remove the lid, add the garlic and sauté for 5 minutes until all the water has evaporated.

Place the cauliflower, garlic, coconut cream and Parmesan cheese or nutritional yeast in the bowl of a food processor and blitz until completely smooth. Season well then transfer to the tart shell and top with the caramelised onion. Scatter over some more thyme leaves and serve immediately.

SEA BASS
WITH BEETROOT & HORSERADISH

SERVES 4

When I lived near Notting Hill in London I would often pop into this amazing local restaurant called Lisa's Kitchen & Bar. The food was so simple and fresh, and most dishes were slathered in horseradish. Beetroot and horseradish is one of my favourite flavour combinations, and the simplicity of the seasoned white fish with these two complementary flavours is a dream. This is a pretty quick meal to knock up if you're in a rush too!

500g raw beetroot, topped and tailed (no need to peel)

2 tsp balsamic vinegar

Olive oil

4 tbsp mayonnaise or Greek yoghurt

50g horseradish, either freshly grated or from a jar, or 2 tsp wholegrain mustard

4 boneless sea bass fillets, skin on

2 tbsp fresh flat-leaf parsley leaves, chopped

Sea salt and freshly ground black pepper

Preheat the oven to 200°C/180°C fan/400°F/Gas mark 6.

Cut the beetroot into 2cm-thick wedges, place in a roasting tray, season well with salt and pepper and toss with the balsamic vinegar and 1½ tablespoons of the olive oil. Roast for 40 minutes until the beetroot is slightly blistered and a sharp knife glides into the thickest part of the flesh without too much resistance.

Meanwhile, combine the mayonnaise or yoghurt and horseradish in a bowl. Season to taste, cover and set aside.

Five minutes before the beetroot is ready, place two pans over a medium–high heat. Drizzle a little olive oil over the sea bass fillets, just enough to coat both sides, and season with salt and pepper. When hot, place 2 fillets in each pan, skin side down. Fry for 3 minutes without moving, then turn over and fry for a further 2 minutes until crisp and golden on both sides.

Plate up the sea bass fillets, sit the beetroot on top and dollop some horseradish on the side. Sprinkle over the parsley and a little drizzle of olive oil and serve immediately.

SPICY MOROCCAN VEGGIE BURGERS

MAKES 5 BURGERS

These sweet and spicy burgers make my mouth water just thinking about them. They're really simple to assemble and don't take long to cook either. The sweet dried apricots are so rich in flavour and give these burgers an exotic taste along with the plethora of spices. If you have a friend or family member who is a big meat-eater and scorns the 'veggie burger', then serve them one of these and watch their attitude quickly change. They're packed with nutritious ingredients too: all-round dreamboat burgers.

1 courgette, coarsely grated

400g tin chickpeas, drained and rinsed

2 tbsp olive oil

8 unsulphured dried apricots

2 cloves garlic, crushed

½ red pepper, deseeded and finely chopped

1 tbsp tomato purée

2 tsp ground cumin

1½ tsp ground coriander

½ tsp ground cinnamon

Grated zest of 1 unwaxed lemon

100g cold cooked quinoa

2 tsp coconut oil

Wholemeal or spelt burger buns or pitta bread, to serve

2 large tomatoes, sliced, to serve

Rocket or lamb's lettuce, to serve

Mayonnaise, to serve (optional)

Sea salt and freshly ground black pepper

Spread the grated courgette out on a chopping board and sprinkle over half a teaspoon of salt. Leave to one side for 10 minutes to degorge.

Put the chickpeas, olive oil and dried apricots in the bowl of a food processor and blitz until almost smooth (some chunks of dried apricots is fine).

Place the courgette in a clean tea towel and squeeze out as much liquid as possible. Add the courgette to a bowl with the chickpea mixture, garlic, red pepper, tomato purée, cumin, coriander, cinnamon, lemon zest, cooked quinoa, half a teaspoon of salt and a good grinding of pepper. Thoroughly combine, taste for seasoning and adjust if necessary. Cover and refrigerate for 20 minutes.

Preheat the oven to 200°C/180°C fan/400°F/Gas mark 6.

Divide the mixture into 5 portions of equal size and shape into burger patties. Add the coconut oil to a pan and set over a medium heat. Fry the burgers for 3 minutes on each side. Transfer to a baking tray and bake in the oven for 15 minutes.

Serve in pitta breads or burger buns with the tomatoes, lettuce and mayonnaise.

STICKY SMOKED PAPRIKA & MAPLE CHICKEN WINGS

SERVES

I served these up for our family on New Year's Eve and my husband and stepkids devoured them with huge grins on their faces. The flavours are sensational and give the chicken a real kick. They're so simple to make as all the work is done during the marinating process. Mix it all up, pop in the fridge and sit back whilst your clever ingredients do all the work.

20 chicken wings, wing tips removed

4 spring onions, finely chopped

4 tbsp maple syrup or honey

2 tbsp tamari or soy sauce

2 tsp smoked paprika

4 cloves garlic, crushed

2cm piece of root ginger, peeled and finely grated

1 tbsp chives, roughly chopped, to serve

Put all of the ingredients, apart from the chives, in a large freezer bag or wide dish and combine until the chicken is completely coated. Close the freezer bag or cover the dish and leave to marinate in the fridge for up to 24 hours – the longer the better. If you are short on time, 2 hours will do.

When you are ready to cook the chicken, preheat the oven to 160°C/140°C fan/ 325°F/Gas mark 3. Transfer the chicken to a roasting pan and cover tightly with foil. Roast for 1 hour, then remove the foil and roast for a further 15 minutes. Remove from the oven.

The chicken can be eaten at this point but, for a delicious char, place a griddle pan over a medium–high heat. Once hot fry the chicken in batches for 1–2 minutes on each side, or just until slightly charred.

Remove to a plate, sprinkle over the chives and serve immediately.

PUY LENTIL, COURGETTE & SWEET POTATO WARM SALAD

SERVES 4

Lentils sometimes get a hard time and can be seen as dull and a bit worthy. I hugely disagree and eat them all the time. They are a great foundation for so many delicious recipes, and the lentils really bring this dish to life. This recipe is vegan and is full of wonderful rainbow veg, from the tomatoes to the carrots and courgettes. Every colour and flavour will benefit your body and health. The lentils are a great dietary fibre so will help your digestion and gut health. With these flavours, you'll never doubt lentils again!

300g puy lentils

Olive oil

2 carrots, peeled, halved lengthways and sliced

2 sweet potato, diced, no need to peel

4 garlic cloves, crushed

1 litre of vegetable stock

1 tbsp coconut or olive oil

2 courgette, sliced lengthways into ½ cm strips

1 tbsp red wine vinegar

1 tbsp soy sauce

3 tbsp extra virgin olive oil

2 tbsp tahini

1 tsp maple syrup

4 tbsp sundried tomatoes, chopped

Sea salt and pepper

Wash the lentils in cold water and drain. Heat two tablespoons of the olive oil in a large pan (with a lid) over a medium heat. Add the carrots and sweet potato and fry for 5 minutes. Add in the garlic and fry for another minute, then add the lentils and vegetable stock. Bring to a boil, then reduce to a simmer, cover and cook for about 25 minutes or until the lentils are tender with a little bite, and have absorbed the majority of the stock.

Meanwhile, heat the coconut oil in a large frying pan over a medium heat, add in the courgette slices and fry for 4 minutes on each side, until golden and softened. Remove to a plate and season well.

When the lentils are done, pour off any excess stock. This can be used again as a stock for soups and stews. While the lentils are still hot season with the red wine vinegar, soy sauce and 1 tablespoon of the extra virgin olive oil.

Combine together the remaining 2 tablespoons of extra virgin olive oil with the tahini and maple syrup. Layer the lentils and courgette onto a serving dish. Drizzle over the tahini dressing and scatter over the sun dried tomatoes.

FLEXI OPTION

Bacon works well with this dish: 6 rashers, roughly chopped and fried with the carrot and sweet potato.

VEGETABLE COUSCOUS

WITH HALLOUMI, MINT & POMEGRANATE

SERVES 2

I adore the colours and flavours of this faux couscous, and I love to serve it with heaps of halloumi and dressing. It's so easy to make and it means you're getting lots of veg in your diet. The mint and pomegranate give this recipe so much flavour and an exotic taste that goes beautifully with the vegetables. This is such a fresh meal for a summer's day.

2 carrots, peeled and chopped

50g radishes

100g cauliflower florets

100g sweet potatoes, chopped (no need to peel)

2½ tbsp olive oil

1 tsp smoked paprika

120g halloumi, sliced

2 tbsp pomegranate seeds

Sea salt and freshly ground black pepper

For the mint yoghurt:

100ml Greek or soy yoghurt

Handful of fresh mint leaves, finely chopped, plus extra to serve

1 clove garlic, crushed

Pinch of sea salt and freshly ground black pepper

To make the mint yoghurt, combine all of the ingredients in a bowl and set aside.

Put the carrots, radishes, cauliflower and sweet potato in the bowl of a food processor and pulse on and off until all the vegetables are finely chopped and roughly the size of couscous. Alternatively, coarsely grate all the vegetables and finely chop.

Put 2 tablespoons of the oil in a pan and set over a high heat. Once hot, add the vegetable couscous and the smoked paprika and fry for 6–8 minutes, stirring regularly, until the vegetables are slightly softened. Season with salt and pepper to taste and leave to one side.

Put the remaining half a tablespoon of oil into another pan and fry the halloumi for 2 minutes on each side until golden.

Plate up the vegetable couscous and top with the halloumi, pomegranate seeds, a scattering of mint leaves and some mint yoghurt. Serve immediately.

If it was more socially acceptable to eat dessert for breakfast, lunch and dinner, I would probably do it. I have a sweet tooth. Actually that doesn't quite cover it: I have twenty-four very sweet teeth. I find it hard to accept that mealtime is over once the savoury part has concluded. It all started growing up in the Cotton household, where Mum loved nothing more than to close the eating ceremony with an ice-cream version of a popular chocolate bar. If we were out of those, a sugary yoghurt or biscuit would do. It is a habit that I've grabbed hold of and run with, as not only does a meal seem strange without dessert, it but I really enjoy it too!

The recipes in this chapter are important as they've given me so much comfort and joy throughout the years. When I first decided to quit refined sugar altogether I knew I would have to tackle my obsession for the sweet stuff head on. The first couple of weeks were strange and disorientating, but after the fog had lifted I felt so much better. I used to quite regularly get a bloated tummy after eating very sugary food, and losing that discomfort was the first positive I noticed. My energy levels are much more balanced these days and I crave sweet things a lot less.

There are, of course, thousands of pieces of research done over the last decade or so about the benefits of losing white sugar from your diet. Ditching it for good will boost your energy levels and make you feel great physically and mentally. For me, it's not a diet or a regime, it's a new way of life that I very much enjoy.

It's not difficult either, as this chapter will testify. I've had the most fun experimenting with recipes in these last two chapters. You can knock up some surprisingly irresistible dishes using natural sweeteners. Coconut sugar, maple syrup and honey are great ingredients for desserts, as are fresh and dried fruit. These are all, of course, still treats, so should be eaten with that in mind, but with these recipes you know exactly what has gone into them and know it's all 100 per cent natural. That's what my body likes!

The Mint-choc ice cream sandwiches (page 182) are welcome to my party any time. The ice cream is divine just on its own, but for a special treat whack it between two home-made choccie biccies and you're flying. My kids love it and are completely unaware it contains spinach. (I'm not sure how long I can get away with that one, but for now I'm sticking with it!) The Banoffee pie (see 179) is dedicated to my husband, who would bathe in the stuff if possible. He tries to avoid refined sugar too, and isn't great with dairy, so this is the perfect version for him.

If like me you dream in chocolate, then get stuck in to this chapter and enjoy every delicious moment.

DESSERTS

ALMOND BUTTER & BANANA SOFT SERVE
WITH STICKY TOFFEE SAUCE

SERVES 2

Give me a bucket of this and a spoon and I'm in heaven. I cannot think of an easier, yummier pudding for when you're in need of comfort and energy. I make this for the kids all the time and they adore it. It's a dream, as it's refined-sugar-free, dairy-free and full of good protein from the nut butter. You could add some cocoa powder to make it chocolaty or some cinnamon to give it some spice. Feel free to make it even more creamy by adding a dollop of soya or coconut yogurt before blending. It tastes so naughty but is so very nice!

4 Medjool dates, pitted and chopped
1 tbsp coconut oil
1 tbsp honey
2 ripe bananas, peeled and frozen
2 tbsp almond butter
Handful of roasted pecan nuts, chopped
1 tbsp goji berries

Put the dates, coconut oil and honey in a saucepan and set over a medium heat. Simmer gently for a few minutes until the coconut oil has melted and the dates are soft and squishy. Transfer to the bowl of a food processor and blitz until smooth. Mix in 2–3 tablespoons of water to thin out the mixture. Transfer to a bowl and rinse out the bowl of the food processor.

Blitz the bananas and almond butter in the food processor until smooth. This may take a few minutes, scraping down the sides at intervals.

Scoop the ice cream into small glasses or bowls and dollop over the date sauce. Top with the pecans and goji berries and serve immediately.

CHOCOLATE RASPBERRY TART

SERVES 10–12

This is the queen of tarts. She stands proudly, bejewelled with raspberries, her chocolaty filling enticing you for just one more slice. It is the most irresistible pudding and will go down a treat with your guests. The crust is light yet sturdy and the filling is dairy-free yet beyond creamy. The crunch of the pastry combined with the creaminess of the filling, topped with the sharp raspberries, makes every bite heavenly. If you don't have coconut cream you can use the thick top layer of tins of coconut milk. Use the watery leftovers in curries, soups or smoothies.

For the pastry:
250g white spelt flour
120g unsalted butter or coconut oil, chilled and cut into small pieces
1 tbsp maple syrup or honey
Sunflower oil, for greasing
¼ tsp fine sea salt

For the filling:
300g coconut cream
¼ tsp vanilla extract
80g coconut palm sugar
300g dark chocolate (minimum 70 per cent cocoa solids), broken into small pieces
50g coconut oil
150g raspberries
Unsweetened cocoa powder, for dusting (optional)

Preheat the oven to 200°C/180°C fan/400°F/Gas mark 6 and grease a 22cm round springform cake tin with a few drops of sunflower oil.

To make the pastry, sift the flour and salt into the bowl of a food processor. Add the chilled butter or coconut oil and blitz until it resembles fine breadcrumbs. Add the maple syrup or honey and 1½–2 tablespoons of water and bring the dough together with your hands until it is in a smooth ball. If it is still crumbly, add a few drops of water at a time, being careful not to overdo it. Flatten the ball, wrap in cling film and refrigerate for 30 minutes until well chilled but still pliable.

Once the pastry has chilled, roll it out between two sheets of floured cling film and use it to line the tart tin. If using coconut oil, you may find the pastry falls apart more easily. If this happens, simply press the pastry directly into the tin, making sure the base and sides are smooth and even with no cracks. Cover and chill in the freezer for 10 minutes. Prick the base of the pastry all over with a fork, line with parchment paper, fill with dry rice or baking beans and blind bake for 20 minutes. Remove the paper and rice or beans and bake for a further 5 minutes until the tart shell is cooked through and biscuity.

To make the filling, put the coconut cream, vanilla extract and sugar in a pan and set over a medium–high heat. Bring to a boil, then reduce the heat immediately and stir until the sugar has dissolved.

Put the dark chocolate pieces and coconut oil in a bowl and pour over the simmering coconut cream mixture. Whisk until the chocolate and coconut oil have melted and come together into a smooth ganache. Pour the mixture into the tart shell and leave to cool, then cover and place the tart in the fridge for at least 3 hours or until very well chilled and set.

Serve the tart with the raspberries tumbled on top and a dusting of cocoa powder, if you like.

BANOFFEE PIE

SERVES 12

This no-bake pie is so fun and easy to make, and will set your taste buds whirring as you spoon large dollops of it into your mouth. It's light yet creamy and decadent, but is free from refined sugar and dairy. Apart from roasting the almonds and heating the banana filling, there is no baking or cooking. Each layer is bursting with flavour and texture and goodness for your body and mind. Good carbs, healthy fats and healing honey and turmeric. Creamy, dreamy and divine.

For the base:
140g raw unsalted almonds
100g oat cakes
130g unsulphured dried apricots
2½ tbsp coconut oil
1 tbsp maple syrup or honey
Sunflower oil, for greasing
Pinch of sea salt

For the filling:
50g coconut oil
7 large ripe bananas, mashed
100g set honey
1 tbsp ground turmeric

For the cream topping:
250ml coconut cream, chilled
1 tbsp set honey
Unsweetened cocoa powder or chocolate shavings, for dusting

Preheat the oven to 180°C/160°C fan/350°F/Gas mark 4 and grease a 22cm round springform cake tin with a few drops of sunflower oil.

Roast the almonds for 5–6 minutes or until a shade darker and aromatic, taking care not let them burn. Leave to cool. Put all the base ingredients in the bowl of a food processor and blitz until the mixture is fine and sticks together when pressed between your fingers. Firmly press the mixture into the base and sides of the tin. Place in the freezer for 10 minutes to set.

To make the filling, add the coconut oil to a pan and set over a medium–low heat. Add the mashed bananas, honey and turmeric and cook gently, stirring regularly, for 20 minutes, until the mixture is rich with a slightly caramelised flavour. Leave to cool, then transfer the mixture to the base of your tart and smooth out.

Combine the coconut cream and honey and spread out over the tart. Cover and refrigerate for at least 1 or 2 hours until set.

When ready to serve, dust with the chocolate shavings or cocoa powder.

SUMMER CITRUS ICE

SERVES 4

This is my kids' new favourite dessert and it couldn't be easier to make. The rosemary infuses the orange juice with such intensity and gives this recipe an extra layer of unexpected flavour. It's a perfect summer pudding, or a little afternoon palette cleanser on a hot day!

4 large sprigs of fresh rosemary (keep a few leaves aside, to serve)

700ml orange juice

Grated zest and juice of 1 unwaxed lemon

4 tbsp maple syrup or honey

Put all the ingredients in a saucepan and bring to the boil for 1 minute. Reduce the heat and simmer for 5 minutes. Remove and leave to cool, then strain through a sieve, squeezing out any liquid from the rosemary.

Transfer the liquid to a shallow metal tray and place it in the freezer. After an hour or two, using a fork, drag the ice crystals into the centre, away from the edges. Repeat after another hour, then leave it in the freezer for another 1–2 hours until completely set.

When ready to serve, remove from the freezer and scrape with a fork to create large, rough crystals – this will take a bit of effort as the liquid will be fully set. Spoon into chilled glasses and serve with the remaining rosemary leaves on top.

MINT-CHOC ICE CREAM SANDWICHES

MAKES 4 ICE CREAM SANDWICHES

I don't drink much these days, so my way of relaxing or feeling a little decadent is eating dessert. It doesn't get much more lavish than these ice cream sandwiches, which ooze creaminess and flavour and look so very naughty. They're very easy to make and I promise you'll get hooked on the mint-choc ice cream and will never buy it from a shop again. The ice cream is great for vegetable-dodging kids too: they can't taste the spinach, but it's most certainly in there, doing their bodies a world of good. The all-round good-guy pud.

3 very ripe bananas, peeled, sliced and frozen

15g fresh mint leaves

6 spinach leaves (optional)

25g dark chocolate (minimum 70 per cent cocoa solids)

8 biscuits (see Rex's Favourite Choccie Biccies p102, or shop-bought)

Put the frozen bananas, mint, spinach, if using, and dark chocolate in the bowl of a food processor and blitz for a few minutes, scraping down the sides now and again, until you have a smooth, soft ice cream.

You can use the ice cream straight away if it is firm enough. However, if it is too soft, transfer it to a Tupperware box and place in the freezer for up to half an hour until it holds its shape.

To serve, scoop one ball of ice cream on to the underside of one of the biscuits. Top with a second biscuit and gently press down so that the ice cream squeezes out of the sides of the sandwich.

Serve immediately.

RICE PUDDING
WITH STICKY PLUMS

SERVES 4

This is the most delightful winter warmer that'll comfort your every cell. It's dairy-free, for those of you who are lactose-intolerant, and so sweet without the help of refined sugar. It's the perfect afternoon treat, and we've tucked into this many times after coming back from cold family walks. The spices and zest give it a real kick, and the juice from the plums makes this dessert even more succulent. It's a challenge not to have seconds straightaway!

For the rice pudding:
150g risotto rice (Carnaroli or Arborio)
400ml tin coconut milk
500ml milk (almond, rice or dairy)
1 tsp vanilla extract
½ tsp ground cinnamon
Good pinch of grated nutmeg
3 tbsp maple syrup or honey
Pinch of sea salt

For the sticky plums:
400g plums, halved and stone removed
1 vanilla pod, halved lengthways
1 cinnamon stick
Peeled zest of 1 unwaxed lemon
100ml orange juice

To serve:
Toasted flaked almonds
Coconut cream

Preheat the oven to 190°C/170°C fan/375°F/Gas mark 5.

Rinse the rice under running water, then put in a pan with the coconut milk and almond, rice or dairy milk and bring to the boil. Reduce the heat to low and simmer gently for 25–35 minutes, stirring regularly to ensure the rice does not stick to the bottom of the pan, until the rice is cooked through with a thick and creamy consistency. Stir in the vanilla extract, cinnamon, nutmeg, salt and maple syrup or honey to taste. Taste and adjust with a little more of any of the ingredients you particularly like.

Meanwhile, put the plum halves, halved vanilla pod, cinnamon stick, lemon zest and orange juice in a roasting tray and bake in the oven for 20–25 minutes until the plums are soft and golden but just holding their shape.

Serve the rice pudding in bowls with the plums on top and a little dollop of coconut cream and some flaked almonds scattered over.

MINI PUMPKIN PIES

MAKES 6 MINI TARTS

I was so happy to hear that so many of you enjoyed my Mini Coconut & Cherry Tarts from my first cookbook, so I set out to create some other mini delights that would be as tasty and easy to make. I love the fun of Halloween and I adore pumpkins, so I experimented with them until these pies evolved one autumnal day. They're filling, yet so light, and don't leave you with a huge sugar high as there is no refined sugar in these mini beauts!

For the base:
100g raw unsalted cashew nuts
90g oat cakes
90g dates, pitted
1 tbsp coconut oil
2 tsp maple syrup or honey
Sunflower oil, for greasing
Pinch of sea salt

For the filling:
550g pumpkin or butternut squash, peeled, deseeded and chopped
2 tbsp coconut oil
1 tbsp set honey
2 tsp ground cinnamon, plus extra for dusting

For the topping:
2½ tbsp cream cheese or coconut cream
1 tsp honey

Preheat the oven to 200°C/180°C fan/400°F/Gas mark 6 and line a six-hole muffin tray with cling film.

Roast the cashews for 5–6 minutes or until a shade darker and aromatic, taking care not let them burn. Leave to cool. Put all the base ingredients in the bowl of a food processor and blitz until the mixture is fine and sticks together when pressed between your fingers.

Press the base mixture into the six lined muffin holes very firmly. Place in the freezer to set for 20 minutes. Remove the tray and carefully lift up the cling film from each hole to release the mini tart cases. Place on a plate, cover and refrigerate for at least 30 minutes.

To make the filling, put the pumpkin or butternut squash pieces and the coconut oil in a pan (with a lid) and set over a low–medium heat. Sweat down the pumpkin or squash for 20 minutes until a knife glides into the flesh easily. Try not to remove the lid too often as it releases the steam.

Once cooked, transfer the pumpkin or squash pieces, leaving behind the oil, to the bowl of a food processor. Add the honey and cinnamon and blitz until smooth. Lleave to cool, then divide the mixture between the 6 tart cases. Cover and refrigerate for at least an hour until chilled and set.

To serve, mix together the cream cheese or coconut cream with the honey. Place one teaspoon of the mixture on top of each mini pie and dust with more cinnamon.

SALTED CARAMEL CHOCOLATE SLICES

MAKES 10-12 SQUARES

This was a request/demand from my husband. When I gave up refined sugar for good, I felt bereft by the lack of chocolate in my life. Then I started to play around with my own homemade stuff and realised that I could modify some of my favourite recipes to leave out the sugar. This post-dinner treat is so moreish and luxurious but has no refined sugar. All the sweetness comes from the juicy dates and maple syrup and the richness from the cacao powder and coconut oil. There is quite a bit of natural sugar in these beauts, so you should still think of them as a cheeky treat!

For the base:
150g raw unsalted almonds
100g dates, pitted
1 tbsp coconut oil
Pinch of sea salt

For the Medjool date caramel:
200g Medjool dates, pitted
50g almond butter
2 tbsp coconut oil, melted
2 tbsp maple syrup or honey
¼ tsp sea salt

For the chocolate topping:
75g cacao butter
40g raw cacao powder or unsweetened cocoa powder
45ml maple syrup or honey
Sea salt, for sprinkling

Grease a 24 x 16cm cake tin and line the base with baking parchment. Put all the base ingredients in the bowl of a food processor and blitz until everything is very finely ground and sticks together when pressed between your fingers. Firmly press the mixture into the cake tin. Place in the freezer for 15 minutes to set.

To make the date caramel, blitz the Medjool dates and 4 tablespoons of water to a smooth paste in a food processor. Add the almond butter and blitz for a couple of seconds until just combined. Add the coconut oil, maple syrup or honey and salt and blitz for another few seconds until incorporated. Don't blitz for any longer as the coconut oil will split away from the oil in the nuts. Maple syrup causes nut butter to seize and become thicker, so don't worry if it becomes firm. Add this to the base and level out with the back of a spoon dipped in boiling water. Cover and place in the freezer while you make the chocolate layer.

For the chocolate layer, melt the cacao butter in a heatproof bowl placed over a pan of simmering water, making sure the base of the bowl does not come into contact with the water. Once melted, remove from the heat and whisk in the cacao powder or cocoa powder and maple syrup or honey until smooth. Pour the chocolate over the date caramel, tapping the tin once or twice on your work surface to make sure it is evenly distributed. Sprinkle over sea salt crystals and leave to set in the fridge for a few hours. Slice into squares and devour!

HEALTHY CHRISTMAS PUDDING

SERVES 8

It's always tough finding a Christmas pudding since my husband doesn't drink (and most puds are laced with booze) and I try to avoid refined sugar: hence the invention of this next chap. There is so much tantalising juice in this pudding, as it's bursting with orange juice and dried fruit. The flavours are pure Christmas and seem to linger on your tongue for ever. If you've never made a Christmas pud from scratch before, maybe now's your time to shine!

Grated zest and juice of 1 orange

200g dates, pitted and chopped

200g unsulphured dried apricots, chopped

100g raisins

100g sultanas

150g coconut oil, melted

2 tbsp orange juice

2 eggs, beaten

100ml milk (almond, rice or dairy)

150g white spelt flour or gluten-free flour

1 tsp baking powder

100g coconut palm sugar

100g spelt or gluten-free breadcrumbs

50g ground almonds

Yoghurt (Greek, soy or coconut) or ice cream, to serve

Redcurrants and holly leaves, to garnish (optional)

Preheat the oven to 180°C/160°C fan/350°F/Gas mark 4. Grease a 1.5-litre pudding bowl and line the base with baking parchment.

Put all the pudding ingredients in a large bowl and mix together until thoroughly combined.

Pour the mixture into the greased and lined pudding bowl and cover the bowl with foil. Put the bowl in a high-sided roasting tray and pour in enough boiling water to come halfway up the side of the bowl.

Cover the bowl and roasting tray with one layer of baking parchment and one layer of foil. Tightly secure the parchment and foil with string so that steam cannot escape. Carefully transfer the tray to the oven and bake for 2½ hours until the pudding feels firm to the touch. Take great care removing the tray from the oven as the water will be boiling hot.

Leave the pudding to cool for 15 minutes, then turn out on to a plate. Garnish with redcurrants and holly leaves and serve with yoghurt or ice cream.

If you are making the pudding in advance, leave it to cool completely in its pudding bowl. Keep it covered in an airtight container and reheat just before serving.

STRAWBERRY CHEESECAKE

SERVES 12

There is no baking needed for this dreamy, fruity cheesecake and if you use maple syrup instead of honey it's completely vegan! The nutty base gives this pudding a deliciously crunchy and warming flavour, and combines really well with the tart fruitiness of the strawberries. The coconut cream brings the middle layer to life as it gives it a luxurious texture and flavour that your friends and family will adore.

For the base:
140g macadamia nuts
80g dried unsulphured apricots
1 tbsp coconut oil
Pinch of sea salt

For the filling:
400g raw unsalted cashew nuts, soaked overnight in cold water
Grated zest of 2 unwaxed lemons
180g honey or maple syrup
50g coconut cream
100g coconut oil, melted
1 tsp vanilla extract
120g strawberries, hulled
½ tsp sea salt

For the strawberry purée:
200g strawberries, hulled, plus more to decorate the top
2 tbsp coconut oil, melted

To serve:
Small handful of fresh mint leaves

Grease a 23cm round springform cake tin. Place all the base ingredients in the bowl of a food processor or in a high-speed blender and blitz until everything is very finely ground and sticks together when pressed between your fingers. Firmly press the mixture into the greased cake tin. Place in the freezer for 15 minutes to set.

Drain the cashew nuts and blitz to a paste in the bowl of a food processor or high-speed blender. Add the rest of the filling ingredients and blitz until everything is thoroughly combined. Pour over the set base and smooth out. Cover and return to the freezer.

For the purée, rinse out the food processor bowl or the blender, add the 200g strawberries and blitz until smooth. Pour into a bowl through a fine sieve, discarding any seeds. Add the melted coconut oil to the strawberry purée and combine. Pour over the cheesecake, smooth out and return to the freezer for at least 4 hours or overnight.

Before serving, remove the cheesecake from the freezer and leave to thaw for about 45 minutes, or until you can cut into it without too much resistance. Serve the cheesecake with more strawberries tumbled on top and the mint scattered over.

Store the cheesecake in an airtight container in the freezer for up to a month, just remember to remove it 45 minutes prior to serving.

APPLE & BLUEBERRY CRUMBLE

SERVES 6

My nan, Ruby, was very fond of a crumble and used to make it for us grandkids whenever we went over for tea. There's something really cathartic and comforting about following this recipe, as it's a really nostalgic dish for me. I've of course swapped the vast quantities of sugar my nan would use for a smaller quantitity of coconut palm sugar and loads more scrummy fruit. The juicy apples and blueberries bubble beneath the crunchy crumble, making this the ultimate pudding for a glorious night in.

For the crumble:
65g white spelt flour
50g extra virgin coconut oil
65g rolled oats
50g coconut palm sugar
½ tsp ground cinnamon
¼ tsp ground nutmeg
Pinch of sea salt

For the filling:
500g bramley apples, peeled, cored and cut into quarters
300g blueberries
80g coconut palm sugar
1 tbsp white spelt flour

Yoghurt (Greek, soy or coconut), to serve

Preheat the oven to 200°C/180°C fan/400°F/Gas mark 6.

For the crumble topping, rub the flour into the coconut oil until you have gravel-sized lumps. Add the oats, coconut palm sugar, cinnamon, nutmeg and salt and mix together. Set aside.

Put the apple quarters and blueberries in a large bowl and combine with the sugar and flour. Transfer to a medium-sized pie dish and top with the crumble (don't press down). Bake for 20–25 minutes until golden brown. Leave to cool for 5 minutes then serve immediately with yoghurt.

Give me a wooden spoon and a set of scales and I'm as happy as a peach in cream. Baking to me is bliss. One of life's simple pleasures that can get me out of a bad mood in minutes as well as filling our house with heavenly vanilla notes and a thunderous noise of rumbling tummies. Each small step of baking a cake requires a certain level of concentration that takes you away from anything else going on outside of your baking circle. It's so therapeutic and calming, with the huge added bonus of having a slab of cake to dive in to afterwards.

I adore that it has become a family ritual that we can all enjoy. My kids grip hold of their spoons for dear life as they keenly mix and spill creamy cake mixture, knowing they'll get to lick the remains afterwards.

Usually cake is seen as a naughty treat that will send your blood sugar level sky-rocketing, with a sliver of guilt thrown into the mix. But these bakes have a slightly more saintly side, as they are all made with unrefined sugars and a lot of love. Some are also made with spelt flour, which is slightly easier on the gut, and some with rice flour, which is gluten-free.

You'll even find a bit of veg lurking in this chapter, in my Beetroot cupcakes (page 198). They taste decadent and rich yet are packed with veg. Win-win! You'll also see there is often the option to use coconut butter instead of dairy butter if you are baking for someone who's lactose intolerant.

My friends come to my house knowing they'll be given cake whether they want it or not, so all of these bakes have been road-tested by many happy customers during the making of this book. The Date & apple squares (page 206) are perfect for the family as they're a dreamy treat that kids love too, and the Upside-down tangerine cakes (page 210) look so pretty – they make the perfect tea-party centrepiece. I hope your loved ones enjoy them just as much as mine do!

BAKED
GOODIES

BEETROOT CUPCAKES

MAKES 10 CUPCAKES

As a parent of young kids I'm always looking for new ways to get veg in their diet. Cakes seem to be a pretty cunning way as they don't look like their natural form or taste like them. Genius! These cupcakes are very pretty as they pick up some of the mighty beetroot's colour, as well as taking on some of the vegetable's natural sweetness. The yoghurt gives them a certain lightness and the cream cheese topping adds a luxurious creamy finish. Make your way towards your five a day in a rather exciting way!

60g unsalted butter

100g coconut palm sugar

1 egg

140g spelt flour

½ tsp bicarbonate of soda

1 tsp baking powder

1 tsp vanilla extract

100g coconut or soy yoghurt

100g cooked beetroot, coarsely grated

For the icing:

1 tbsp beetroot juice, squeezed out of 2 tbsp finely grated raw beetroot

100g cream cheese, or dairy-free alternative

2 tbsp set honey

Desiccated coconut or chocolate shavings, for sprinkling (optional)

Preheat the oven to 180°C/160°C fan/350°F/Gas mark 4 and line a cupcake tray with 10 paper cases.

Place the butter and sugar in a large bowl and cream together until light and fluffy. Beat in the egg, flour, bicarbonate of soda, baking powder and vanilla extract until combined. Fold in the yoghurt and grated beetroot until thoroughly combined.

Divide the mixture between the cupcake cases and bake for 16–18 minutes. Remove from the oven and leave to cool.

Meanwhile, combine the beetroot juice, cream cheese and honey. (If you are using dairy-free cream cheese that is quite runny, reduce the honey so the mixture remains thick.) Once the cupcakes have cooled, spoon on the cream cheese and sprinkle over the desiccated coconut or chocolate shavings, if using.

TRIPLE-TIER CHOCOLATE & ORANGE CAKE

SERVES 10–12

Chocolate cake is the most requested in our house; the kids and Jesse love it. The dark chocolate gives the cake its depth and luxury and the orange gives it a zesty kick. The honeyed oranges on top make this cake look spectacular, so although it takes a bit of effort it's a real show stopper if you have guests. This could also be a really good birthday cake for a loved one who likes to eat cake yet avoid refined sugar.

For the orange crisps:
1 orange, very thinly sliced
80ml honey

For the cake:
180g coconut palm sugar
5 eggs
180g coconut oil or unsalted butter, melted
190g ground almonds
50g white spelt flour
1½ tsp bicarbonate of soda
1½ tsp baking powder
Grated zest of 1 orange
150g dark chocolate (70 per cent cocoa solids), melted
¼ tsp sea salt

For the icing:
100g set honey
500g cream cheese, or dairy-free alternative
Grated zest of 2 oranges
100g coconut oil, melted

Preheat the oven to 120°C/100°C fan/250°F/Gas mark ½. Line a baking tray with baking parchment, and grease three 20cm round cake tins and line with baking parchment.

Put the orange slices and honey in a pan with 250ml of water and bring to the boil. Reduce the heat and simmer for 25–30 minutes until the orange slices are translucent. Drain and delicately lay them on the lined baking tray. Bake for 1½ hours until dry but pliable. Leave to cool and increase the oven temperature to 180°C/160°C fan/350°F/Gas mark 4.

For the icing, beat together the honey and a quarter of the cream cheese until combined. Beat in the remainder of the cream cheese and zest until barely combined. Do not over-beat or it may become runny. Stir in the melted coconut oil until it becomes smooth and thick. Cover and refrigerate.

To make the cake, whisk together the sugar, eggs and salt until it has doubled in volume. In another bowl combine the melted coconut oil or butter, ground almonds, flour, bicarbonate of soda and baking powder. Fold in the orange zest, melted chocolate, and egg and sugar mixture until well combined. Divide the mixture between the three cake tins. Bake for 15–18 minutes, until firm to the touch and a skewer inserted into the centre of a cake comes out clean. Turn out on to a wire rack and leave to cool.

Ice the top of one cake with a third of the icing, then place the second cake on top and ice with another third of the icing. Finally add the third cake and top with the remaining icing. Decorate the top with the orange crisps.

CARROT CAKE TRAY BAKE

SERVES 10

Another request from my husband Jesse and one that is much devoured by all of us in the Wood household. Who doesn't love a carrot cake? This tray bake is an all-time classic to serve up to hungry visitors who pop over for tea, or to be selfishly eaten on your own with massive mugs of tea! It is again another wonderful way to get some veg in your diet in a really delicious way.

225g white spelt flour

2 tsp baking powder

1½ tsp ground cinnamon, plus extra for sprinkling

½ tsp ground nutmeg

1 tsp ground ginger

60g raisins

3 eggs, beaten

180g coconut oil, melted

120g coconut palm sugar

360g carrots, peeled and coarsely grated

2 oranges, zest of 1 and peel of the other

Pinch of sea salt

For the icing:

250g cream cheese, or dairy-free alternative

2 tbsp set honey

Preheat the oven to 200°C/180°C fan/400°F/Gas mark 6 and line a 28 x 20cm tray bake tin with baking parchment.

In a large bowl, mix together the flour, baking powder, cinnamon, nutmeg, ginger, raisins and salt. In a separate bowl, combine the eggs, melted coconut oil, coconut palm sugar, carrots and the grated zest.

Add the wet mixture to the dry flour mixture and thoroughly combine. Pour this into the cake tin and smooth out. Bake in the oven for 30–40 minutes until golden and until a skewer inserted into the centre comes out clean. Cover with foil if it is browning too quickly. Remove from the oven and leave to cool for 20 minutes, then carefully remove the cake and leave to cool completely on a wire rack.

Meanwhile, combine the cream cheese and honey. (If you are using dairy-free cream cheese that is quite runny, reduce the honey so the mixture remains thick.) Once the cake is cool, spread the icing over the cake. Finely slice the orange peel and sprinkle over. Store in an airtight container for up to 5 days.

CHOCOLATE, ALMOND & COURGETTE LOAF CAKE

SERVES 8-10

Loaf cakes are so satisfying to make due to the glorious and cathartic simplicity of the process – and the vast quantity of cake there is as a result! This chocolate loaf is so rich, yet retains a certain lightness due to the hidden courgette. Another great way to get one of your five a day in, and another sneaky route to ensure your kids do too. It is still a treat, of course, so don't substitute it for your kid's main meal! My husband likes to take this one to band rehearsals with him for tea breaks. The perfect teatime slab of cake!

100g coconut oil or unsalted butter, at room temperature

150g coconut palm sugar

2 eggs, beaten

225g courgette, coarsely grated

3 tbsp almond milk

150g white spelt flour

50g ground almonds

1 tsp baking powder

1 tsp bicarbonate of soda

1½ tsp ground cinnamon

4 tbsp unsweetened cocoa powder

1 tsp vanilla extract

½ tsp fine sea salt

To decorate (optional):

50g dark chocolate, melted, for drizzing

Flaked almonds, to decorate

Preheat the oven to 180°C/160°C fan/350°F/Gas mark 4. Grease a 20 x 10cm loaf tin and line with baking parchment.

In a large bowl cream together the coconut oil and sugar until light and fluffy, then gradually beat in the eggs, courgette and milk until well combined.

In another bowl combine the remaining ingredients. Gradually add this to the coconut oil and sugar mixture, until it has just come together. Don't over-mix as it will make the cake tough.

Transfer the mixture to the lined loaf tin and bake for 45–55 minutes, or until a skewer inserted into the centre of the cake comes out clean. If the top is browning too quickly, cover with foil. Cool in the tin for 10 minutes, then transfer to a wire rack to cool completely.

Decorate with the flaked almonds and the dark chocolate drizzled over.

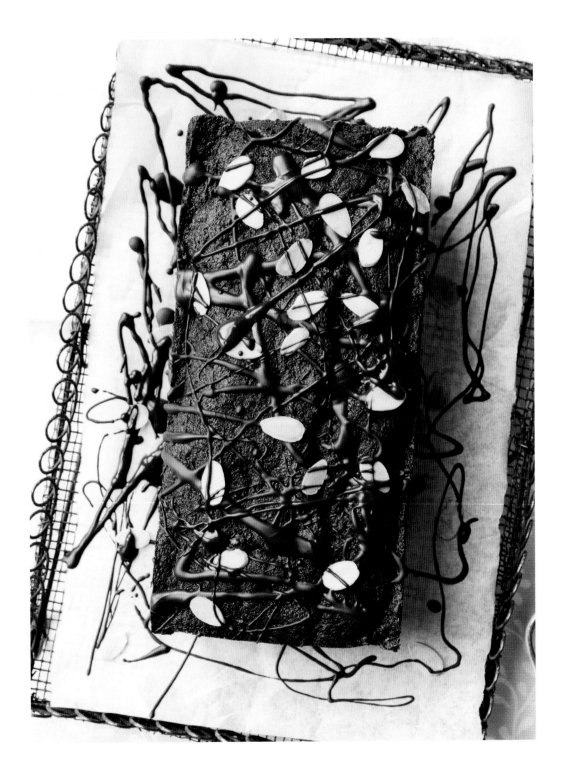

DATE & APPLE SQUARES

MAKES 10–12 SQUARES

You're getting a whole load of fibre in these sweet squares, as the dates and apple will work magic on your digestive system. There's a little spice in there to awaken your taste buds and a nice chew due to the fruit and oats. These are really fun to make with the kids as they're simple and have delicious results. A comforting treat to serve whilst still warm, or a delicious bite to devour at any point of the day when you need a little pick-me-up and down time.

150g apple, grated
140g dates, pitted and chopped
¼ tsp ground cinnamon
250g rice flour or white spelt flour
100g coconut palm sugar
1 tsp bicarbonate of soda
90g porridge oats
210g unsalted butter or coconut oil, or a combination of the two, melted
40g flaked almonds
Ice cream or yoghurt, to serve
Pinch of sea salt

To serve (optional):
Ice cream
Yoghurt

Preheat the oven to 200°C/180°C fan/400°F/Gas mark 6 and line a 24 x 16cm bake tin with baking parchment.

Put the grated apple, chopped dates and 160ml of water in a pan (with a lid) and bring to the boil. Immediately turn the heat to low, put the lid on and simmer very gently for 10 minutes. Remove the lid and continue to simmer for another 5–10 minutes until the apple and dates are completely soft and all of the water has evaporated, leaving a sticky (but not wet) mixture.

Add the mixture to the bowl of a food processor with the cinnamon and blitz until smooth. Transfer to a bowl and leave to one side.

In a bowl combine the flour, coconut palm sugar, bicarbonate of soda, oats, salt and melted butter and/or coconut oil until it all comes together into a ball of dough.

Press half of the dough into the base of the lined cake tin, compacting it into the four corners. Spread the date and apple mixture on top, then spread out the remaining dough evenly over the top. Scatter the flaked almonds over the surface and lightly press down to secure them in place.

Bake in the oven for 20–25 minutes until golden, then remove and leave to cool completely. Cut into squares and serve them as they are or with a scoop of ice cream or some yoghurt. Store in an airtight container for up to 3 days.

EASTER LEMON CAKE

SERVES 10

I need no particular celebration to bake or eat cake, but Easter seems like a good enough excuse to put a bit more time and effort into making an extra special one. It's so beautiful to look at and deliriously gorgeous to eat, but I love the baking process most with this one. The lemons and ground almonds give the cake a wonderfully moist texture and the honey naturally sweetens it perfectly. Happy Easter!

150g ground almonds
150g white spelt flour
1 tsp baking powder
1 tsp bicarbonate of soda
Grated zest of 2 unwaxed lemons
180ml clear honey
5 eggs
180g coconut oil or unsalted butter, melted

For the icing:
4 tbsp set honey
500g cream cheese, or dairy-free alternative
Grated zest of 2 unwaxed lemons
2 tbsp coconut oil or unsalted butter, melted

To decorate (optional):
Mini chocolate eggs and mini baby chicks

Preheat the oven to 180°C/160°C fan/350°F/Gas mark 4 and grease two 18cm round cake tins and line with baking parchment.

To make the icing, beat together the honey and a quarter of the cream cheese until combined. Beat in the remainder of the cream cheese, zest and melted coconut oil or butter until barely combined. Do not over-beat or it may become runny. (If you are using dairy-free cream cheese that is already quite runny, reduce the honey so the mixture remains thick.) Cover and refrigerate.

In a bowl, combine the ground almonds, flour, baking powder, bicarbonate of soda and lemon zest. In a separate bowl whisk together the honey, eggs and melted coconut oil or butter. Pour this into the dry mixture and combine.

Divide the cake mixture between the two cake tins and bake for 25–30 minutes, or until a skewer inserted into the centre of the cakes comes out clean. Cover with foil if they brown too quickly. Remove and leave to cool for 15 minutes, then turn out on to a wire rack to cool completely.

Once the cakes are cool, with a serrated knife level off each sponge by cutting off the uneven tops, so that you are left with two perfectly flat cakes. Keep the cut-off sponge for snacking on.

Ice the top of one cake with a quarter of the icing, then top with the second cake and do a crumb coating. To do this, take another quarter of the icing and coat the top and sides of the cake sparingly, so that the 'crumb' of the cake is now coated in a thin layer of icing, sealing in the crumbs. Refrigerate for 30 minutes to set the crumb coating.

With the remaining icing, ice the top and sides of the cake as you did before, but this time creating a thick and even layer of icing over the entire cake (a palette knife dipped in hot water is useful for this). Refrigerate for another hour to set the icing.

When ready to serve, decorate with the mini chocolate eggs and baby chicks, if using.

UPSIDE-DOWN TANGERINE CAKES

MAKES 6 MINI CAKES

One of my favourite places to take the kids is Kew Gardens in London. It's loads of fun – and to top it off the café there serves up really great cakes and treats. One of my favourites is their upside down orange cake, so I wanted to create my own version for this book that didn't contain refined sugar. My daughter, Honey, and step-daughter, Lola, both love tangerines, so I used them for the top of these cakes as they look so pretty and are the right size for a smaller bake. Fruity and sweet but tangy and fresh, these cakes make the most delicious little treat.

120g coconut oil or
unsalted butter
120g coconut palm sugar
2 eggs, beaten
Grated zest of 1 orange
120g white spelt flour
2 tsp baking powder
2 tbsp honey
2 tangerines, sliced
Yoghurt (Greek, soy or coconut),
to serve

Preheat the oven to 200°C/180°C fan/400°F/Gas mark 6 and grease six darioles or pudding moulds.

In a large bowl cream together the coconut oil or butter and the sugar until light and fluffy. Beat in the eggs one by one. Fold in the zest, flour and baking powder.

Divide the honey between the 6 moulds and place one slice of tangerine in the bottom of each mould with the honey. Pour over the sponge mixture and bake for 15–17 minutes until they have risen and are golden. A skewer inserted into the centre of one of the cakes should come out clean.

Remove from the oven and leave to cool for 2 minutes, then turn out on to plates and serve with a dollop of yoghurt.

PEANUT BUTTER & JAM CUPCAKES

MAKES 10 CUPCAKES

Peanut butter and jam go together like duvets and books. Total soul-satisfying perfection. I eat a lot of nut butter as I adore the creaminess and flavour and am always happy to boost up my daily protein with it too, so getting my fave ingredient into a bake was a must for this book. The jam is a little hidden secret inside that will be delightfully discovered when bitten in to, and the creamy topping just makes these little dream boats even more decadent. Serve up when your mates or family drop over for tea, or give to your little ones as a cheeky treat.

60g unsalted butter or coconut oil

120g coconut palm sugar

60g smooth peanut butter

2 eggs, beaten

120g white spelt flour

2 tsp baking powder

2 tbsp milk (almond, rice or dairy)

For the raspberry chia jam:
200g raspberries, plus extra to serve

2 tbsp honey

2½ tbsp chia seeds

For the icing:
250g cream cheese, or dairy-free alternative

80g smooth peanut butter

40g honey

Preheat the oven to 180°C/160°C fan/350°F/Gas mark 4 and line a cupcake tin with 10 paper cases.

To make the jam, add the raspberries and honey to a pan and set over a medium heat. Simmer for 5 minutes, mashing the raspberries to release their liquid. Stir in the chia seeds and continue to simmer for 15 minutes until thick and viscous. Remove from the heat and leave to cool.

Meanwhile, in a large bowl cream together the butter or coconut oil and sugar until light and fluffy. Beat in the peanut butter and eggs, then fold in the flour, baking powder and milk. Divide the mixture between the paper cases and bake for 16–20 minutes until risen and golden. A skewer inserted into the centre of a cupcake should come out clean.

Leave to cool for 10 minutes, then transfer to a cooling rack and leave to cool completely (otherwise the icing will melt).

To make the icing, combine the cream cheese, peanut butter and honey until smooth. Cover and refrigerate until needed.

Once the cupcakes have cooled, cut out a small thumb-size hole from the centre of each one. (The excess bits of cake can be eaten as a snack while you assemble your cupcakes!)

Fill each hole with a teaspoon of the raspberry chia jam. Keep any remaining jam in a jar in the fridge. Top each cupcake with a tablespoonful of the icing, then position a raspberry on top of each one.

WHOLEMEAL CAKE WITH FRUIT

SERVES 10-12

This cake is wholesome, hearty and simple. It reminds me of the countryside due to its rustic appearance and fruity finish. The ground almonds and spelt flour give the cake texture and also reduce its gluten-content (as the almonds contain none and the spelt contains very little). The yoghurt and fruit add a simple and fresh topping to this wholesome cake. Serve in delightful slabs and don't worry about the presentation. That is the beauty of this haphazard bake.

225g unsalted butter or coconut oil

250g coconut palm sugar

1 tsp vanilla extract

4 eggs, beaten

150g wholemeal spelt flour

150g ground almonds

1½ tsp baking powder

For the topping:

150g yoghurt (Greek, soy or coconut)

250g fruit of your choice (I have used blackberries, kiwis and strawberries here)

1 tbsp toasted flaked almonds

1 tbsp honey, for drizzling

Preheat the oven to 180°C/160°C fan/350°F/Gas mark 4. Grease and line a 20cm round cake tin.

Cream together the butter or coconut oil and the sugar until light and fluffy. Beat in the vanilla extract and the eggs, one by one, then fold in the flour, ground almonds and baking powder.

Pour the cake mixture into the tin and bake for 50–60 minutes, or until a skewer inserted into the centre of the cake comes out mostly clean. Cover with foil if it is browning too quickly. Remove from the oven and leave to cool for 10 minutes, then turn out on to a wire rack and leave to cool completely.

When you are ready to serve, top with the yoghurt, fruit and flaked almonds and drizzle over the honey. Alternatively, the yoghurt can be served on the side.

INDEX

Afternoon Pick-me-up Ginger Citrus Smoothie
  114
Afternoon Treats 98
  Afternoon Pick-me-up Ginger Citrus Smoothie
  112, 114
  Cashew, Chia & Cranberry Brittle 100–101
  Chocolate Milk 113, 115
  Raw Carrot & Chia Bites 116–17
  Raw Flapjacks 104–5
  Rex's Favourite Choccie Biccies 102–3
  Savoury Popcorn 108–9
  Simple Afternoon Tea Biscuits 110–11
  Soothing Ginger & Turmeric Tea 120–21
  Sweet Potato Scones 106–7
  Vanilla, Oatmeal & Walnut Loaf Cake 118–19
almond butter 26–27, 32–33, 66–67, 106–7,
  116–17, 174–75, 188–89
Almond Butter & Banana Soft Serve 174–75
Almond, Chia & Goji Flapjacks 38–39
almond milk 9
Afternoon Treats 113, 118–19
  Baked Goodies 204–5, 212–13
  Breakfast recipes 14, 15, 18–19, 25
  Desserts 184–85, 190–91
  Elevenses 36–37
almonds
  Baked Goodies 200–201, 204–5, 206–7,
    208–9, 214–15
  Desserts 178–79, 184–85, 188–89, 190–91
  Elevenses 38–39, 42–43
  Food to Share 150–51, 153
  Soups & Salads 68–69, 70–71
anchovies 74
Apple & Blueberry Crumble 194–95
apple juice 44–45
apples 44–45, 48–49, 131, 194–95, 206–7
Apricot Buckwheat Porridge 14, 16–17
apricots, unsulphured 11, 14, 26–27, 44–45,
  164–65, 178–79, 190–91, 192–93

Asian Fried Rice 136–37
Asian Marinated Tofu 90–91
asparagus 86–87, 140–41
aubergines 96–97, 128–29, 150–51
Avocado Cream 46–47
avocados
  Breakfast recipes 25
  Elevenses 40–41, 46–47
  Family Favourites 124–25, 130, 142–43
  Lunch on the Run 84–85, 88–89
  Soups & Salads 66–67

Baked Aubergine 150–51
Baked Cabbage & Apple 131
Baked Cod, Aubergine & Tomatoes 128–29
Baked Goodies 196
  Beetroot Cupcakes 198–99
  Carrot Cake Tray Bake 202–3
  Chocolate, Almond & Courgette Loaf Cake
    204–5
  Date & Apple Squares 206–7
  Easter Lemon Cake 208–9
  Peanut Butter & Jam Cupcakes 212–13
  Triple-tier Chocolate & Orange Cake 200–
    201
  Upside-down Tangerine Cakes 210–11
  Wholemeal Cake with Fruit 214–15
Balsamic & Red Pepper Hummus 48–49
bananas
  Afternoon Treats 112, 113
  Breakfast recipes 18–19, 24, 25, 32–33
  Desserts 174–75, 178–79, 182–83
  Elevenses 42–43
Banoffee Pie 178–79
bean sprouts 52–53
beans 64–65, 70–71, 94–95, 126–27, 156
Beetroot, Chickpea & Quinoa Soup 54–55
Beetroot Cupcakes 198–99
beetroots 54–55, 68–69, 162–63, 198–99

berries *see specific type*
biscuits 102–3, 110–11, 182–83
blueberries 18–19, 32–33, 42–43, 194–95
Blueberry & Banana Muffins 42–43
breakfast bars 26–27
Breakfast recipes 12
    Apricot Buckwheat Porridge 14, 16–17
    Buckwheat Crepes 18–19
    Carrot Cake Porridge 15, 16–17
    Cocoa, Chia, Kale & Oat Breakfast Smoothie
       24
    Courgette & Sweet Potato Hash 28–29
    Frozen Latte 25
    Fruity Breakfast Omelette 32–33
    Multi-seed Breakfast Bars to Go 26–27
    Peach Breakfast Crumble 22–23
    Rosemary and Date Spelt Loaf 20–21
    Scrambled Eggs 30–31
    Strawberries & Cream Porridge 15, 16–17
    Strawberry, Avocado & Hemp Smoothie 25
Broad Bean & Mint Topping 156–57
broccoli 52–53, 60–61, 78–79
brown rice syrup 26–27, 100–101
buckwheat 10, 14, 17, 18–19
Buckwheat Crepes 18–19
buffalo mozzarella 78–79, 132–33, 144–45
burgers 164–65
butternut squash 72–73, 142–43, 146–47, 155,
   157, 186–87
Butternut Squash & Kale Warming Salad 72–73
Butternut Squash Rings 155, 157

cabbage, red 131
cacao butter 188–89
cacao powder 10, 102–3, 188–89; *see also* cocoa
   powder
cakes
    Beetroot Cupcakes 198–99
    Carrot Cake Tray Bake 202–3
    Chocolate, Almond & Courgette Loaf Cake
       204–5
    Easter Lemon Cake 208–9
    Ginger & Lemon Loaf Cake 36–37
    Peanut Butter & Jam Cupcakes 212–13

    Strawberry Cheesecake 192–93
    Triple-tier Chocolate & Orange Cake 200–201
    Upside-down Tangerine Cakes 210–11
    Vanilla, Oatmeal & Walnut Loaf Cake 118–19
    Wholemeal Cake with Fruit 214–15
cannellini beans 94–95
capers 74
Carrot, Avocado & Tofu Salad 66–67
Carrot Cake Porridge 15, 16–17
Carrot Cake Tray Bake 202–3
Carrot Noodles 153, 154–55
carrots
    Afternoon Treats 116–17
    Breakfast recipes 15, 16–17
    Family Favourites 126–27, 142–43
    Food to Share 150–51, 153, 154–55, 170–71
    Lunch on the Run 78–79
    Soups & Salads 54–55, 58–59, 66–67
    Cashew, Chia & Cranberry Brittle 100–101
cashew cream 15
cashew nut butter 48–49, 116–17
cashews 26–27, 62–63, 100–101, 142–43,
   150–51, 158–59, 186–87, 192–93
cauliflower 80–81, 152, 154, 160–61, 170–71
Cauliflower-rice-stuffed Tomatoes 80–81
celery 131
chia seeds 11
    Afternoon Treats 100–101, 116–17
    Baked Goodies 212–13
    Breakfast recipes 22–23, 24, 26–27
    Elevenses 38–39, 44–45
chicken 56–57, 138–39, 158–59, 166–67
chickpeas 48–49, 54–55, 60–61, 164–65
chillies, red 52–53, 56–57, 62–63, 92–93,
   136–37
chives 54–55, 58–59, 82–83, 138–39, 166–67
Chocolate, Almond & Courgette Loaf Cake
   204–5
chocolate, dark 104–5, 176–77, 182–83,
   200–201, 204–5
Chocolate Milk 113, 115
Chocolate Raspberry Tart 176–77
Christmas Pudding 190–91
Cinnamon Apple Balls 44–45

cocoa powder
  Afternoon Treats 102–3, 104–5, 113
  Baked Goodies 204–5
  Breakfast recipes 24, 25
  Desserts 176–77, 178–79, 188–89
coconut cream 9
  Breakfast recipes 15, 18–19, 30–31
  Desserts 176–77, 178–79, 184–85, 186–87, 192–93
  Family Favourites 146–47
  Food to Share 160–61
Coconut-crusted Haddock Fingers 134–35
coconut, desiccated 26–27, 104–5, 116–17, 134–35
coconut flour 66–67
coconut milk 9, 56–57, 138–39, 184–85
coconut oil 8
coconut palm sugar 9
coconut yoghurt 198–99
cod fillets 128–29
coffee 25
Cook Happy, Cook Healthy (Cotton) 11
corn cobs 73, 157
Courgette & Sweet Potato Hash 28–29
Courgette Balls 153, 154–55
courgettes
  Baked Goodies 204–5
  Breakfast recipes 28–29
  Family Favourites 130
  Food to Share 153, 154–55, 164–65, 168–69
  Lunch on the Run 78–79, 84–85, 86–87
  Soups & Salads 70–71
cranberries, dried 100–101
cream cheese 36–37, 186–87, 198–99, 200–201, 202–3, 208–9, 212–13
cream, dairy 30–31
Creamy Leeks 146–47
crème fraiche 82–83
crumbles 22–23, 194–95
cucumbers 46–47, 82–83, 142–43
curry 138–39

dairy alternatives 9; see also almond milk; coconut milk; nut butters; oat milk; rice milk

Date & Apple Squares 206–7
dates 11
  Afternoon Treats 104–5, 113, 116–17
  Baked Goodies 206–7
  Breakfast recipes 20–21, 24
  Desserts 174–75, 186–87, 188–89, 190–91
  Elevenses 44–45
Desserts 172
  Almond Butter & Banana Soft Serve 174–75
  Apple & Blueberry Crumble 194–95
  Banoffee Pie 178–79
  Chocolate Raspberry Tart 176–77
  Healthy Christmas Pudding 190–91
  Mini Pumpkin Pies 186–87
  Mint-choc Ice Cream Sandwiches 182–83
  Rice Pudding 184–85
  Salted Caramel Chocolate Slices 188–89
  Strawberry Cheesecake 192–93
  Summer Citrus Ice 180–81
dressings 62–63, 66–67, 74, 75, 94–95
dried fruits and seeds 11
drinks 25, 114, 115, 120–21

Easter Lemon Cake 208–9
egg dishes 28–29, 30–31, 32–33
Elevenses 34
  Almond, Chia & Goji Flapjacks 38–39
  Avocado Cream 46–47
  Balsamic & Red Pepper Hummus 48–49
  Blueberry & Banana Muffins 42–43
  Cinnamon Apple Balls 44–45
  Ginger & Lemon Loaf Cake 36–37
  Guacamole Cracker Snacks 40–41
  Oil-free Hummus & Veg Sticks 48–49

Family Favourites 122
  Asian Fried Rice 136–37
  Baked Cabbage & Apple 131
  Baked Cod, Aubergine & Tomatoes 128–29
  Coconut-crusted Haddock Fingers 134–35
  Healing Vegan Stew 126–27
  Jesse's Fish Sarnie 124–25
  Paradise Chicken Curry 138–39
  Quick & Healthy Pizza 132–33

Roast Butternut Squash 146–47
Salmon Tray Bake 140–41
Squash, Carrot & Cucumber Risotto 142–43
Super-simple Veggie Tray Bake 130
Sweet Potato Pasta Salad 144–45
feta 48–49, 64–65, 84–85, 130, 150–51
Fig & Green Bean Salad 64–65
fish 82–83, 94–95, 128–29, 134–35, 140–41,
    162–63
flapjacks 38–39, 104–5
flax seeds 116–17
flours and grains 10–11
Food to Share 148
    Baked Aubergine 150–51
    Butternut Squash Rings 155, 157
    Courgette Balls 153, 154–55
    Parsnip Rostis 156
    Puy Lentil, Courgette & Sweet Potato Warm
        Salad 168–69
    Red Onion & Cauliflower Tart 160–61
    Roast Chicken, Cashew & Chilli Salad 158–59
    Sea Bass 162–63
    Smokey Cauliflower 152, 154
    Spicy Moroccan Veggie Burgers 164–65
    Sticky Smoked Paprika & Maple Chicken Wings
        166–67
    Vegetable Couscous 170–71
Fried Asparagus & Courgette Chip Salad 86–87
Frozen Latte 25
Fruity Breakfast Omelette 32–33

Get Well Soon Soup 60–61
Ginger & Lemon Loaf Cake 36–37
Ginger & Lime Tofu Noodle Salad 62–63
ginger, root
    Afternoon Treats 112, 120–21
    Elevenses 36–37
    Family Favourites 136–37, 138–39
    Food to Share 158–59, 166–67
    Lunch on the Run 92–93
    Soups & Salads 52–53, 56–57, 62–63
goat's cheese 30–31, 70–71
goji berries 11, 38–39, 104–5, 174–75
green beans 64–65

Guacamole Cracker Snacks 40–41

haddock fillets 124–25, 134–35
halloumi 170–71
Healing Vegan Stew 126–27
Healthy Christmas Pudding 190–91
hemp seeds 25
honey 9–10
horseradish 162–63
Hot Smoked Salmon Open-faced Sandwich
    82–83
Hummus 48–49, 58–59, 124–25

ice cream 174–75, 182–83

Jesse's Fish Sarnie 124–25

kale 24, 60–61, 72–73, 126–27, 157
kidney beans 126–27

leeks
    Family Favourites 142–43, 146–47
    Food to Share 150–51
    Lunch on the Run 78–79, 80–81, 84–85
    Soups & Salads 54–55, 58–59, 70–71
lemongrass 56–57, 62–63
lemons/juice/zest
    Afternoon Treats 112, 120–21
    Baked Goodies 208–9
    Desserts 180–81, 184–85, 192–93
    Elevenses 36–37, 46–47, 48–49
    Family Favourites 124–25, 128–29, 134–35
    Food to Share 153, 156, 164–65
    Lunch on the Run 88–89, 94–95
    Soups & Salads 68–69, 74, 75
Lentil Winter Warmer Soup 58–59
lentils 58–59, 168–69
lettuces 64–65, 82–83, 124–25, 142–43,
    164–65
limes/juice/zest 40–41, 52–53, 56–57, 62–63,
    112, 136–37, 158–59
Lunch on the Run 76
    Asian Marinated Tofu 90–91
    Cauliflower-rice-stuffed Tomatoes 80–81

Fried Asparagus & Courgette Chip Salad
   86–87
Hot Smoked Salmon Open-faced Sandwich
   82–83
Leek & Courgette Pasta 78–79
Prawn, Avocado & Lemon Mayo Wrap 88–89
Rainbow Stir-fry 92–93
Smoked Tofu, Aubergine & Spinach 96–97
Stuffed Avocados 84–85
Tuna & Cannellini Bean Lunchbox Salad 94–95

macadamia nuts 192–93
mange tout 92–93
mangos 62–63
maple syrup 10
milk (almond, rice or dairy) 14, 18–19, 25, 36–37,
   118–19, 184–85, 190–91, 212–13
Mini Pumpkin Pies 186–87
Mint-choc Ice Cream Sandwiches 182–83
Mint Yoghurt 170–71
mixed fruits and berries 214–15
mixed leaves 88–89, 158–59
molasses 36–37
mozzarella 78–79, 80–81, 132–33, 144–45, 153
Multi-seed Breakfast Bars to Go 26–27
Mushy Peas 134–35

nectarines 22–23, 86–87
nut butters 9, 48–49, 116–17, 212–13
nutritional yeast 86–87, 150–51, 156, 160–61
nuts see specific type

oat cakes 178–79, 186–87
oat milk 9, 24, 26–27, 113
oats
   Afternoon Treats 100–101, 104–5, 118–19
   Baked Goodies 206–7
   Breakfast recipes 15, 22–23, 24, 26–27
   Desserts 194–95
   Elevenses 38–39
Oil-free Hummus & Veg Sticks 48–49
oils and sauces 8–9
olive oil 8
onions 52–53, 126–27, 138–39, 153

onions, red
   Breakfast recipes 28–29
   Family Favourites 136–37, 140–41, 142–43
   Food to Share 158–59, 160–61
   Lunch on the Run 94–95
   Soups & Salads 58–59, 60–61, 62–63
oranges/juice/zest
   Afternoon Treats 112
   Baked Goodies 200–201, 202–3, 210–11
   Breakfast recipes 15
   Desserts 180–81, 184–85, 190–91
   Soups & Salads 68–69

Paprika & Maple Chicken Wings, Sticky Smoked
   166–67
Paprika & Tahini Dressing, Smoked 75
Paradise Chicken Curry 138–39
Parmesan cheese 86–87, 96–97, 150–51, 156,
   160–61
Parsnip Rostis 156
passata 126–27
pasta 10–11, 78–79, 144–45
Peach Breakfast Crumble 22–23
peanut butter 116–17, 212–13
Peanut Butter & Jam Cupcakes 212–13
peanuts 62–63
peas 134–35
pecans 144–45, 174–75
peppers, fresh red 92–93, 94–95, 164–65
peppers, mixed 130
peppers, roasted red 30–31, 48–49, 96–97,
   144–45, 155, 157
pesto 132–33, 150–51
pies and tarts, savoury 160–61
pies and tarts, sweet 176–77, 178–79, 186–87
pine nuts 130, 146–47
Pizza 132–33
plums 184–85
pomegranate seeds 157, 170–71
popping corn 108–9
porridge 14–17
potatoes, new 140–41
Prawn, Avocado & Lemon Mayo Wrap 88–89
prawns 88–89, 92–93, 136–37

Pumpkin Pies, Mini 186–87
pumpkin seeds 15, 22–23, 26–27, 40–41
Puy Lentil, Courgette & Sweet Potato Warm
    Salad 168–69

Quick & Healthy Pizza 132–33
quinoa 10
    Family Favourites 126–27, 138–39
    Food to Share 157, 164–65
    Lunch on the Run 78–79
    Soups & Salads 54–55, 68–69, 72–73

radishes 30–31, 170–71
Rainbow Stir-fry 92–93
raisins 15, 190–91, 202–3
raspberries 176–77, 212–13
Raw Carrot & Chia Bites 116–17
Raw Flapjacks 104–5
Red Onion & Cauliflower Tart 160–61
Rex's Favourite Choccie Biccies 102–3
rice 10–11
    Desserts 184–85
    Family Favourites 136–37, 138–39, 142–43
    Food to Share 150–51
    Lunch on the Run 90–91, 92–93
rice flour 10, 42–43, 102–3, 134–35, 206–7
rice milk 9
    Afternoon Treats 118–19
    Baked Goodies 212–13
    Breakfast recipes 14, 15, 18–19, 25, 26–27
    Desserts 184–85, 190–91
    Elevenses 36–37, 42–43
rice noodles 52–53, 62–63
rice, puffed 26–27
Risotto, Squash, Carrot & Cucumber 142–43
Roast Butternut Squash 146–47
Roast Chicken, Cashew & Chilli Salad 158–59
rocket
    Family Favourites 124–25, 132–33, 142–43
    Food to Share 164–65
    Lunch on the Run 82–83, 86–87, 94–95
    Soups & Salads 62–63, 64–65
Rosemary and Date Spelt Loaf 20–21
Runner Bean Salad 70–71

Salads 50
    Butternut Squash & Kale Warming Salad
        72–73
    Carrot, Avocado & Tofu Salad 66–67
    Fig & Green Bean Salad 64–65
    Fried Asparagus & Courgette Chip Salad
        86–87
    Ginger & Lime Tofu Noodle Salad 62–63
    Puy Lentil, Courgette & Sweet Potato Warm
        Salad 168–69
    Roast Chicken, Cashew & Chilli Salad 158–59
    Runner Bean Salad 70–71
    Salsa Verde 74
    Simple Summer Beetroot & Orange Salad
        68–69
    Smoked Paprika & Tahini Dressing 75
    Sweet Potato Pasta Salad 144–45
    Tuna & Cannellini Bean Lunchbox Salad 94–95
salmon 82–83, 140–41
Salmon Tray Bake 140–41
Salsa Verde 64–65, 74
Salted Caramel Chocolate Slices 188–89
sandwiches 82–83, 88–89, 124–25
Savoury Popcorn 108–9
Scrambled Eggs 30–31
Sea Bass 162–63
seeds see specific type
sesame seeds, toasted 66–67, 90–91, 92–93,
    153
shallots 62–63
Simple Afternoon Tea Biscuits 110–11
Simple Summer Beetroot & Orange Salad
    68–69
Smoked Paprika & Tahini Dressing 75
Smoked Tofu, Aubergine & Spinach 96–97
Smokey Cauliflower 152, 154
soba noodles 60–61, 96–97
Soothing Ginger & Turmeric Tea 120–21
Soups 50
    Beetroot, Chickpea & Quinoa Soup 54–55
    Get Well Soon Soup 60–61
    Lentil Winter Warmer Soup 58–59
    Thai Coconut Soup 56–57
    Veggie Vietnamese Soup 52–53

soy yoghurt 170–71, 198–99
spelt flour 10
    Afternoon Treats 106–7, 110–11, 118–19
    Baked Goodies 198–99, 200–201, 202–3,
       204–5, 206–7, 208–9, 210–11, 212–13,
       214–15
    Breakfast recipes 18–19, 20–21, 22–23
    Desserts 176–77, 190–91, 194–95
    Elevenses 36–37, 40–41, 42–43
    Family Favourites 132–33
    Food to Share 160–61
    Lunch on the Run 86–87
Spicy Moroccan Veggie Burgers 164–65
spinach leaves 30–31, 68–69, 90–91, 96–97,
    113, 138–39, 144–45, 182–83
spring onions 52–53, 90–91, 136–37, 153,
    166–67
Squash, Carrot & Cucumber Risotto 142–43
stew 126–27
Sticky Plums 184–85
Sticky Smoked Paprika & Maple Chicken Wings
    166–67
Sticky Toffee Sauce 174–75
stir-fries 92–93
store cupboard 8–11
    dairy alternatives 9
    dried fruits and seeds 11
    flours and grains 10–11
    oils and sauces 8–9
    sweet things 9–10
strawberries 15, 16–17, 18–19, 25, 192–93
Strawberries & Cream Porridge 15, 16–17
Strawberry, Avocado & Hemp Smoothie 25
Strawberry Cheesecake 192–93
Stuffed Avocados 84–85
sugar, coconut 9
sultanas 190–91
Summer Citrus Ice 180–81
sunflower seeds 14, 26–27, 116–17
Super-simple Veggie Tray Bake 130
Sweet Potato Pasta Salad 144–45

Sweet Potato Scones 106–7
sweet potatoes 28–29, 58–59, 60–61, 106–7,
    126–27, 144–45, 168–69, 170–71
sweetcorn 60–61, 72–73, 157
sweeteners 9–10

tahini 8–9, 40–41, 46–47, 48–49, 72–73, 75,
    168–69
tamari 8, 90–91, 92–93, 136–37, 142–43, 153,
    166–67
tangerines 210–11
Thai Coconut Soup 56–57
Toffee Sauce, Sticky 174–75
tofu 52–53, 62–63, 66–67, 90–91, 96–97
tomatoes
    Family Favourites 128–29, 130, 132–33,
       140–41
    Food to Share 164–65
    Lunch on the Run 78–79, 80–81, 84–85,
       86–87, 94–95
tomatoes, sun-dried 82–83, 168–69
Triple-tier Chocolate & Orange Cake 200–201
Tuna & Cannellini Bean Lunchbox Salad 94–95

Upside-down Tangerine Cakes 210–11

Vanilla, Oatmeal & Walnut Loaf Cake 118–19
Vegetable Couscous 170–71
Veggie Vietnamese Soup 52–53

walnuts 25, 44–45, 118–19
Wholemeal Cake with Fruit 214–15

yeast, fast-action 132–33
yoghurt
    Baked Goodies 198–99, 210–11, 214–15
    Breakfast recipes 22–23
    Desserts 190–91, 194–95
    Elevenses 48–49
    Food to Share 162–63, 170–71
    Lunch on the Run 82–83, 88–89

ACKNOWLEDGEMENTS

At this final point of the book, I feel an urgent rush of gratitude flowing through the floodgates. What a joy it is to have had the opportunity to write and create a second cookbook. I'm bursting with love and thanks.

Firstly thank YOU for bothering to read the acknowledgements as well as my pretty little book. I do hope you have enjoyed making, baking and reading your way through its pages. For me, seeing your creations on social media and hearing your feedback is so thrilling. Keep cooking, eating and loving!

Orion, you incredible gang of individuals. Thank you for kick-starting my cookbook career and for having such faith to publish me in the first place. Amanda Harris and Emily Barrett, you are heavenly to work with. Thanks for receiving emails at 6:30am pondering recipe selection and front cover font. I appreciate every bit of help and guidance!

Jordan Bourke you Irish dream. How lucky am I that I got to work with you again! You have helped me refine and perfect my recipes and ideas and are always willing to hear out my flavour concoctions and creations. Your time and energy are so appreciated and I hope we get to do this all over again soon.

Rowan Lawton at Furniss Lawton, can you believe chatting about our favourite subject – FOOD – is actually pertinent to our careers? Jammy! Thanks for helping me get cookbook number two off the ground and for all your advice along the way.

Huge love and eternal thanks to Mary, Rachel, Claire and Sarah at James Grant for keeping me on track, listening to me be hugely indecisive and for telling me what the hell I'm supposed to be doing each day. Without you I'd be a mess. A golden team of wonderful women!

Thank you Tamin Jones for once again making the food look celestial on the pages of this book. Your delicate touch photographing these dishes has made this book exactly what I had hoped for. Liam Arthur, thanks for such fun days taking photos of me cooking and eating. The shots of me and Rex were especially fun and ones I will cherish forever. The cover is just as I had imagined. Bright, fun and very, very pink!

Rebecca Newport, can I please have your job! You have once again selected the most glorious crockery, backdrops and colours for the food to sit upon. Total kitchen heaven! Thank you! Briony Hartley, thank you for bringing all of these ideas and fragments together to make sense as a book.

The biggest gratitude-swamped hugs for my darling friend, Jessie May. Your illustrations have a fairytale quality that make me feel comforted every time I look at them. Thanks for once again letting your imagination run wild.

Justine Jenkins, Lisa Eastwood and Sinead Mckeefry (aka Sue) – you girls are the BEST! Thanks for making me look less like a tired, rushed-off-my-feet mumma and more like a well-scrubbed domestic queen. You had your work cut out for you. Endless gossiping and so much fun whilst getting ready for these shoots.

Thank you to my husband, Jesse, and my kids and stepchildren Arthur, Lola, Rex and Honey – you total beauts. Thanks for your helping hands in the kitchen and your hungry mouths to try out my recipes. I adore your very honest feedback; you are my most adored guinea pigs.

I still get a buzz thinking that I've had this chance to write a second cookbook, so thanks again for giving this book a go – I'm chuffed to bits! Now get out of my kitchen as I've got a lot of tidying up to do.

THANKS!

First published in Great Britain in 2017
by Orion Publishing Group Ltd

Carmelite House, 50 Victoria Embankment
London, EC4Y 0DZ

An Hachette UK Company

10 9 8 7 6 5 4 3 2 1

Text © Fearne Cotton 2017
Design and layout © Orion Publishing Group Ltd 2017

A CIP catalogue record for this book
is available from the British Library.

ISBN: 9781409169437

Author photography: Liam Arthur
Food photography: Tamin Jones
Design: Briony Hartley
Illustrations: Jessica May Underwood
Props: Rebecca Newport
Recipe development and food styling: Jordan Bourke

Printed in Germany

*Note: While every effort has been made to ensure
that the information in this book is correct, it should
not be substituted for medical advice. It is the sole
responsibility of the reader to determine which foods
are safe to consume. If you are concerned about any
aspect of your health, speak to your GP.*

The Orion Publishing Group's policy is to use
papers that are natural, renewable and recyclable
products and made from wood grown in sustainable
forests. The logging and manufacturing processes
are expected to conform to the environmental
regulations of the country of origin.

www.orionbooks.co.uk

For more delicious recipes,
features, videos and exclusives
from Orion's cookery writers,
and to sign up for our 'Recipe
of the Week' email visit
bybookorbycook.co.uk

With thanks to Cath Kidston, Anthropologie,
Le Creuset, Elanbach, Osborne and Little, RICE,
Rebecca Newport Textiles, Rockett St George,
Melody Rose and Wallpaper Direct.